Wildflowers of
Shenandoah National Park

Facts and Information
Shenandoah National Park

History
Established: December 26, 1935
Visitors: about 1,100,000 annually

Physical Features
Acreage: 197,438 acres including 79,570 acres designated wilderness
Elevation: lowest point: 561 feet near north end; highest point: 4,049 feet at Hawksbill
Water resources: over 90 streams; highest waterfall: Overall Run at 93 feet
Average precipitation: 40–50 inches annually
Temperature range: -10° to 100°
Plants: 1,400+ species of plants including 862 species of wildflowers 267 species of trees and shrubs; 95% of park forested
Animal species: about 200 birds; 50 mammals; 32 fish; 27 reptiles; 24 amphibians including 1 federally endangered salamander

Facilities
Entrance stations: North Entrance at Front Royal; Thornton Gap near Luray, Swift Run Gap near Elkton, and Rockfish Gap at Waynesboro
Roads: 105 mile long Skyline Drive plus accessory roads; 1 tunnel: Marys Rock Tunnel at 12' 8"; 75 overlooks; Mileposts: on west side of Skyline Drive beginning with 0 at Front Royal to 105 at Waynesboro
Trails: 516 miles of trails including 101 miles of Appalachian Trail and 200 miles of designated horse trails
Campgrounds: 4 campgrounds with 647 sites
Picnic areas: 7

Wildflowers of Shenandoah National Park

A Pocket Field Guide

Ann and Rob Simpson

FALCONGUIDES

Guilford, Connecticut

Helena, Montana
An imprint of Globe Pequot Press

FALCONGUIDES®

Copyright © 2011 by Morris Book Publishing, LLC
All photos © Ann and Rob Simpson/www.snphotos.com

FalconGuides is an imprint of Globe Pequot Press.

Falcon, FalconGuides, and Outfit Your Mind are registered trade-
marks of Morris Book Publishing, LLC.

Half-title page photo: bloodroot, *Sanguinaria canadensis*
Title page photo: blue-eyed grass, *Sisyrinchium angustifolium*

Library of Congress Cataloging-in-Publication Data is available on
file.

ISBN 978-0-7627-6436-5

Printed in China
10 9 8 7 6 5 4 3 2 1

Contents

Eastern Redbuds and Flowering Dogwoods greet spring visitors to Shenandoah National Park.

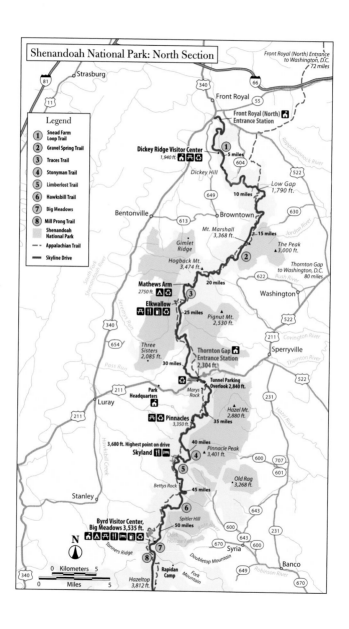

Shenandoah National Park: North Section

Legend

1. Snead Farm Loop Trail
2. Gravel Spring Trail
3. Traces Trail
4. Stonyman Trail
5. Limberlost Trail
6. Hawksbill Trail
7. Big Meadows
8. Mill Prong Trail

- Shenandoah National Park
- - - Appalachian Trail
— Skyline Drive

Front Royal (North) Entrance to Washington, D.C. 72 miles

Strasburg

Front Royal

Front Royal (North) Entrance Station

Dickey Ridge Visitor Center
1,940 ft.
—5 miles

Dickey Hill

Low Gap
1,790 ft.

10 miles

Brownton

Bentonville

Mt. Marshall
3,368 ft.
15 miles

The Peak
▲3,000 ft.

Gimlet Ridge

Hogback Mt.
3,474 ft.▲

Thornton Gap to Washington, D.C. 80 miles

20 miles

Mathews Arm
2750 ft.

Elkwallow

—25 miles

Pignut Mt.
2,530 ft.

Washington

Three Sisters
2,085 ft.

Pass Run

30 miles

Thornton Gap Entrance Station
2,304 ft.

Sperryville

Park Headquarters

Tunnel Parking Overlook 2,840 ft.

Marys Rock

Luray

Pinnacles
3,350 ft.

Hazel Mt.
2,880 ft.

35 miles

3,680 ft. Highest point on drive

Skyland

40 miles

Pinnacle Peak
▲3,401 ft.

Old Rag
3,268 ft.

Bettys Rock

45 miles

Stanley

Spitler Hill

Byrd Visitor Center, Big Meadows 3,535 ft.

50 miles

Syria

Banco

N

Tanners Ridge

Hazeltop
3,812 ft.

Rapidan Camp

Fork Mountain

Doubletop Mountain

Kilometers 5

Miles 5

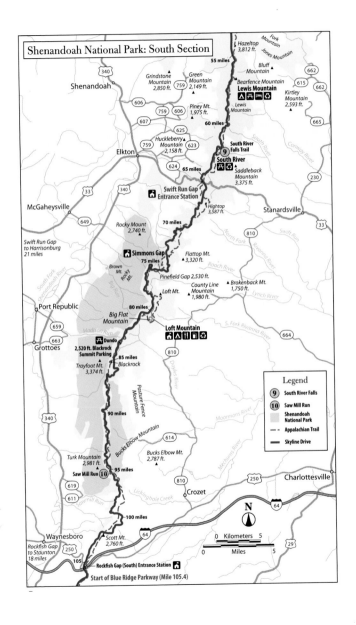

Shenandoah National Park: South Section

Acknowledgments

Many thanks to the faithful park personnel of Shenandoah National Park who have dedicated their lives to preserving the natural resources of the park and sharing the wonders of Shenandoah's wildflowers with visitors. We would especially like to thank Mara Meisel and Wendy Cass for sharing their wealth of botanical knowledge about the park's flora. Our thanks also go to Greta Miller and the staff and members of the Shenandoah National Park Association for their continued support of the interpretative and educational mission of the park. Special thanks go to Becky Gregory, Karen Michaud, Rick Frederick, and Jake Hughes for their special contributions to this book. We would also like to thank all the staff at FalconGuides and Globe Pequot Press, especially Jessica Haberman, whose support and efforts made this National Park wildflower series a reality. We would like to dedicate this book to our family for their love and support, including Rob's

mom, Melba Simpson of Dresden, Ontario, and our children and their spouses, Jeremiah, Mitzi, Jessie, Roger, Aaron, Chelo, and Jamie. We especially dedicate this book to our marvelous grandchildren, Georgia, Gracie, and Jacob, who constantly remind us about the joy of wildflowers and the innocent amazement of the wonders of the natural world.

The Shenandoah National Park Association

The large-flowered trillium is the logo for the Shenandoah National Park Association.

The Shenandoah National Park Association (SNPA) is a private, non-profit organization whose sole purpose is to provide support to the interpretive and educational activities of Shenandoah National Park, achieved primarily through the sales of educational books, maps, DVDs, and other items on the human and natural history of the park. The profits from the sales of these items in the two visitor centers and through mail order are used to fund various programs and activities managed by the Interpretive Division of the park.

Membership in SNPA is open to the public and offers the opportunity to personally support the park as well as receive special discounts on purchases from the Association bookstores. SNPA has a large membership base that continues to support the activities of the Association and the park. More information about SNPA is available online at www.snpbooks.org or by calling (540) 999-3582.

If you plan a visit to Shenandoah, remember to bring along this new wildflower guide to explore!

Introduction

Shenandoah National Park is a fantastic place to enjoy nature and especially the fascinating wildflowers that are found here. From the craggy peaks of Old Rag Mountain to the rolling fields and wet

Meadow of oxeyes and Old Rag Mountain

meadows of Big Meadows, more than 1,400 species of plants can be found in a diversity that typifies the mid-Appalachian Mountains. More than 850 species of wildflowers have been identified in Shenandoah. The intriguing world of wildflower identification can be a great way to add to your enjoyment of the park.

Wildflowers of Shenandoah National Park is an easy-to-use pocketsize field guide to help visitors identify over 125 of the most common wildflowers of the park. Botanical terms have been kept to a minimum, and a color picture accompanies each flower description. Perfectly sized to fit easily into a day pack, this compact field guide is filled with information about each flower, including natural history notes, ethnobotanical uses, and historical uses.

About Shenandoah National Park

For 105 miles, Skyline Drive crests Shenandoah National Park along the Blue Ridge Mountains in Virginia only 75 miles west of Washington, D.C. The fertile Shenandoah Valley lies to the west, and the low rolling foothills of Virginia's Piedmont region lie to the east. Elevations range from 590 feet in the north section to 4,049 feet at Hawksbill summit. Spanning the entire length of the park, the famous Skyline Drive begins at the northern entrance to the park in Front Royal and ends 105 miles later in Waynesboro. The road continues as the Blue Ridge Parkway, a 469-mile scenic highway that ends at Great Smoky Mountains National Park. A section of the Appalachian Mountain chain, the Blue Ridge is an ancient mountain range that stretches from Pennsylvania to Georgia. Every mile along the Skyline Drive is marked with a numbered cement milepost on the west side that is easily seen from the road. Seventy-five well-placed pullouts allow visitors ample opportunities to enjoy the vistas and scenic overlooks.

Four entrances into Shenandoah National Park divide the park into three sections. The north section begins at Milepost 0 at Front Royal and ends at Thornton Gap, forming the division between the north and central section. The central section continues to Swift Run Gap. The south section continues to Milepost 105 at Rockfish Gap. At the average park speed limit of 35 mph, it takes about three hours to travel the entire length of the park on the Skyline Drive. It is always advisable to begin a visit by stopping at one of the park visitor and information centers. Dickey Ridge Visitor Center at Mile 4.7 and Harry F. Byrd Sr. Visitor Center at Milepost 51 offer information and park maps.

The center of park visitor activities is at the Big Meadows area with its restaurants, a lodge, campground, and a camp store. Skyland facilities at Mile 41.7 include lodging, a restaurant, and a gift shop. Three wayside food stops offer sandwiches and basic supplies: Elkwallow Wayside at Mile 24.1, Big Meadows Wayside at Mile 51.2, and Loft Mountain Wayside at Mile 79.5. Four campgrounds offer campsites, some with RV sites: Mathews Arm at Mile 22.1, Big Meadows at Mile 51.2, Lewis Mountain at Mile 57.5, and Loft Mountain at Mile 79.5.

Eastern Redbuds and Flowering Dogwood along Skyline Drive

Visitor services and facilities are typically available March through November. Be sure to check the park website (www.nps.gov/shen) for current opening and closing information. For general park information call (540) 999-3500; for emergencies only call (800) 732-0911.

Where to Find Wildflowers

The Appalachian Trail meanders 101 miles through Shenandoah. Another 400 miles of trails ranging from easy to strenuous

Interrupted Fern glade with Rose Azalea

allow visitors a wide range of hiking opportunities. Several of these trails are especially noted as places to find wildflowers. See Suggested Wildflower Hikes in Shenandoah.

In some cases, the location of wildflowers has been given in the form of habitats where they are typically found. Exact locations of some rare or endangered plants have been omitted to help prevent damage to these valuable species. Wildflower poachers have been known to decimate an entire population of flowers for their personal use or for monetary profit. Many wildflowers do not transplant well and have met their demise at the hands of "flower lovers" who wanted to take a plant home. It is illegal to pick, dig, or harm any plant in a national park. Please leave the plants for others to enjoy and report any suspicious activity to a park ranger.

When to Find Wildflowers

Wildflower season in Shenandoah begins in late March, when the earliest spring bloomers brave the cool mountain temperatures. Spring beauty, hepatica, and Dutchman's breeches grace the forest floor, pushing aside the warm blanket of brown winter leaves. These and other early flowers fade away by the end of April. May brings carpets of white, yellow, and purple violets along the trails. In the central section of the park, especially near the Lewis Mountain area, large-flowered trilliums put on a display of delicate white flowers under the forest canopy. Shrubs of bright pink azaleas begin showing their flowers in late May, followed by the paler pink flowers of mountain laurel in June. July sports pink milkweeds, orange Turk's cap lilies, and yellow sunflowers that provide summer butterflies a sweet nectar treat. Late August and September bring waving goldenrods and purple asters to redecorate the park.

A female ruby-throated hummingbird sips nectar from a cardinal flower.

Fall foliage peaks in late October, when the park explodes with bright-red leaves of Virginia creeper and red maple followed by the brilliant oranges and subdued yellows of oaks, hickories, and tulip trees.

Photography Tips

Lighting and sharp focus are the keys to taking great wildflower photos. Overcast days offer nice soft lighting for wildflowers. In deep shade, increase the ISO or use a flash. Bright, sunny days create harsh shadows, and a flash is needed to add detail to the dark shaded areas of the flowers.

Streaming waterfalls flow through lush vegetation.

When photographing a group of wildflowers, focus on the front of the group. With close-ups, focus about one-third from the front. A macro lens with image stabilization capability will help stop camera motion at high magnifications. For more advanced camera systems, shooting at f16 with a flash will stop motion and provide more depth of field.

When taking wildflower photos, be careful not to trample other plants.

Safety Notes

Always let someone know when you go for a hike. Dress in layers; carry rain gear and plenty of water.

Black bears are common in the park, but most will avoid you if they hear you coming. Never feed wildlife. Not only is it illegal but it also endangers the welfare of the animal.

Copperheads and rattlesnakes are found in the park and are often quite camouflaged, so watch where you put your hands and feet.

Ticks are common throughout the park, so take precautions to prevent bites. Along with insect repellent, wear light-colored

Poison ivy

clothing so that you can see crawling ticks easier, and tuck your pant legs into your socks. Always do a tick check after being outside. Tick bites are painless but may carry a bacterium that causes Lyme disease. Never squeeze a tick to remove it; instead grasp it with tweezers as close as possible to the embedded head and firmly pull the tick straight out. If you develop a rash or flulike symptoms, see your health care provider.

Learn what poison ivy looks like to avoid the irritating rash associated with this plant. Contact may produce an itchy rash caused by an oil called urushiol, present in all parts of the plant. "Leaves of three, let it be" and "hairy vine, no friend of mine" are two adages that warn of the plant's irritating nature. Characterized by having three leaves, poison ivy can grow as a 4-foot-tall shrub or trailing ground cover. Older vines thicken and climb high into trees, sending out hairy rootlets.

Conservation Note

Please leave wildflowers where they grow. When hiking, stay on established trails and watch where you put your feet to avoid damaging plants, especially on rocky outcroppings.

How to Use This Guide

Common and Scientific Name

In an effort to create consistent communication worldwide, each plant has a Latin name, genus, and species that are unique to that plant. Common names of families are given, with the scientific family name in parentheses. In many cases, a plant may have many common names, often varying by locality. Also, genetic research is rapidly changing the taxonomic status of many plants. Taxonomic names used in this guide are consistent with Alan S. Weakley's *Flora of the Southern and Mid-Atlantic States* and the *Flora of Virginia,* to be published in 2012.

Color

The simplest way to begin identification of any wildflower is by color. The color tabs in this book will help you begin the process of identifying a flower. Unfortunately, color is not an exact clue, as some flowers begin their life as one color and gradually change over time. Large-flowered trillium begins life as a pure white flower and as it ages turns pink, sometimes with maroon stripes. In these cases, we recommend searching for the plant name in the index when it is not easily searchable by color.

Height

Average plant heights are given in inches or feet. Variability in plant height can be influenced by many factors. Shaded plants may need to grow larger to reach available sunlight. Cold temperatures and harsh conditions may stunt plants at high altitudes.

Yellow lady's slipper orchids along Skyline Drive

Bloom Season

Plants in this guide are arranged within their flower color by bloom time. For instance, a red flower blooming in early spring will come before a red flower that blooms later in the season. Some plants may have a very specific bloom season, such as bloodroot, which blooms only for few short weeks in early spring. Other plants, like wild columbine, may bloom from spring into fall. The flowering seasons begin earlier and last longer at low elevations. It is generally about 4 degrees cooler for each 1,000 feet in elevation rise.

Flowers in the south section often bloom earlier than those in the north section.

Habitat

Some plants are found throughout the park, while others are only located in a very narrow range. Some plants grow best where there is moist soil, and some plants can survive in very dry conditions. Shade-loving plants like rich forests, and sunbathers like exposed south-facing slopes. Some plants will only grow in a symbiotic relationship with other plants or fungi. North-facing slopes are often much cooler and moister, providing a refuge for boreal plants that are typically found farther north.

Flower and Leaf Shape

The shape of the flowers and leaves can be very helpful in plant identification. Flowers can be single or in multiples. They can be bell shaped, tubular, rounded, or flattened. Leaves may be narrow or broad, long or short, wavy or even lacy.

View into the Shenandoah Valley from Gooney Manor Overlook

Suggested Wildflower Hikes
in Shenandoah

Below are several noteworthy wildflower hikes in the park. Consult a park topographic map or hiking book, such as *Best Easy Day Hikes in Shenandoah National Park* (FalconGuides) by Bert and Jane Gildart, for additional hike details.

1. Snead Farm Loop Trail, Mile 5.1. An easy hike to an old farm site; along the way you can spot wild sarsaparilla, cut-leaved toothwort, bloodroot, and wild geranium.

2. Gravel Spring Trail, Mile 17.6. For this short hike to the Gravel Spring Hut, take the fire road for easy access to see such spring wildflowers as ramps, Jack-in-the-pulpit, Solomon's seal, Indian cucumber, Appalachian meadow rue, and blue cohosh.

Virginia bluebells along Dickey Ridge Trail

3. Traces Trail, Mile 22.2. Wetland plants such as cardinal flower, marsh violet, and marsh marigold are examples of the flowers that can be found along this trail near Mathews Arm Campground.

4. Stonyman Trail, Mile 41.7. This popular trail in the park offers many of the boreal life zone species, such as three-toothed cinquefoil and Michaux's saxifrage, which is an Appalachian endemic.

5. Limberlost Trail, Milepost 43. With the death of the giant hemlock forest caused by a tiny insect called the hemlock woolly adelgid, the Limberlost Trail is seeing rapid succession, with beautiful groves of mountain laurel and woodland flowers such as pink lady's slippers, false hellebore, and an excellent selection of violets.

6. Hawksbill Trail, Mile 46.7. The highest peak in the park is where you can see bluebead lily, Allegheny stonecrop, and trilliums.

7. Big Meadows, Milepost 51. On an easy stroll through a high-elevation meadow, you can see unusual Virginia plants including devil's bit and fly poison. In summer the meadow is filled with colorful flowers such as butter-and-eggs, common milkweed, butterfly milkweed, nodding onion, and lance-leaved goldenrod. Autumn brings warm glows from berry bushes along with yellow ladies' tresses orchids, rough-stemmed goldenrod, and several asters.

8. Mill Prong Trail, Mile 52.8. Rose twisted stalk, northern bush honeysuckle, miterwort, and showy orchis are but a few of the wildflowers along this popular wildflower trail.

Mountain Laurel along the Appalachian Trail at Saw Mill Run

9. South River Falls Trail, Mile 62.8. Enjoy an invigorating hike to a plunging waterfall and along the way take pleasure in numerous spring wildflowers including violets, blue cohosh, wild geranium, Jack-in-the-pulpit, and many other species that occur in rich woods.

10. Saw Mill Run, Mile 95.3. In early spring, wildflowers along this section of the Appalachian Trail are those that like dry, acidic conditions, including trailing arbutus and pygmy pipes. In summer you can find slender ladies' tresses orchids, goat's rue, wild indigo, and whorled coreopsis.

Blue Cohosh

SKUNK CABBAGE

Symplocarpus foetidus
Bloom season: February–April
Arum family (Araceae)
Height: 1–2″

Though not common in Shenandoah, skunk cabbage can be found along Dickey Ridge Trail even before the snow begins to melt. A true hothead, the plant can actually generate heat enough to melt the surrounding snow. Skunk cabbage is appropriately named. Combined with its rotting-flesh odor and putrid-meat color, the flower attracts carrion flies, which are one of the few insects that fly in near-freezing temperatures. Snails are also attracted to the warming bowels of this plant. Even though toxic, Native Americans processed the leaves medicinally to heal wounds.

WILD GINGER

Asarum canadense

Bloom season: April–May

Birthwort family (Aristolochiaceae)

Height: 6–12″

Hiding low to the ground, the rusty-brown bell-shaped flowers of wild ginger are difficult to see under the heart-shaped leaves. With a taste mildly similar to that of ginger spice, which is grown in tropical areas, the dried and powdered root of wild ginger was used by settlers to flavor food, especially meats. The root was also sliced and then cooked in sugary syrup and made into a candy. The leftover syrup was poured on hotcakes. Since then, scientists have discovered that this plant contains aristolochic acid, which may cause cancer, and should not be used as a food source.

JACK-IN-THE-PULPIT

Arisaema triphyllum
Bloom season: April–June
Arum family (Araceae)
Height: 8–24"

The unusual shape of this member of the arum family has engendered many stories that explain its appearance. Tiny yellow flowers are located at the base of a 2-to-8-inch spike called a spadix, which is hidden inside an outer cylindrical leafy structure called a spathe. "Jack" (the spadix) refers to the parson in his arching pulpit (the spathe). Plants are either male or female and can change sex from year to year. If the plant has stored enough nutrients, it will develop female parts and will bear seeds inside bright red berries; otherwise it will remain male. All parts of the plant contain crystals of calcium oxalate, which cause a needlelike burning in the mouth. Young pranksters dubbed the plant "memory plant" after tempting their unknowing visitors into trying a bite.

BLUE COHOSH

Caulophyllum thalictroides
Bloom season: April–June
Barberry family (Berberidaceae)
Height: 1–3′

In the cool air of spring, the dull yellowish-green flowers of blue cohosh bloom before the lobed leaflets are fully open. "Cohosh" comes from an Algonquin word that refers to the rough root. The plant was widely used for women's problems and as an aid during childbirth, generating the nickname papoose root, or squawroot. To ease childbirth, women drank a tea made from dried cohosh roots a few weeks prior to childbirth. As with many plants that are used as folk remedies and herbals, blue cohosh has been a target of illegal plant poachers, which may lead to a scarcity of this early-spring bloomer.

ALUMROOT

Heuchera americana
Bloom season: April–June
Saxifrage family (Saxifragaceae)
Height: 2–3′

Alumroot belongs to the same genus as flowers that are often planted in gardens called coral bells. The small greenish bell-shaped nodding flowers attract small bees for pollination. The broad rounded leaves fan out under the long flower stalks. The Latin name, *Heuchera,* honors an eighteenth-century German physician and botanist, Johann von Heucher. Native Americans used alumroot for many medicinal purposes. The leaves were used as an astringent for sores. After drying, the root was used for stomach pain, diarrhea, and other bowel complaints.

SMOOTH SOLOMON'S SEAL

Polygonatum biflorum
Bloom season: May–June
Ruscus family (Ruscaceae)
Height: 12–36″

Two rows of small bell-shaped greenish-white to cream-colored flowers hang delicately from the long arching green stem of smooth Solomon's seal. The flower was named to honor King Solomon, whose wisdom was widely proclaimed, including his knowledge of herbal uses. The horizontal underground stem, or rhizome, has marks that resemble the wax seal used on important documents. Believed to have magical powers, it was used as a love potion and to ward off evil spirits. Native Americans ate the prepared rhizomes, a good source of starch, like potatoes. They also used it medicinally to apply to bruises and to treat dysentery and lung diseases.

FALSE HELLEBORE

Veratrum viride
Bloom season: May–July
Bunchflower family (Melanthiaceae)
Height: 2–8'

Growing in wet woodlands and swampy areas, false hellebore, or green false hellebore, frequently towers above its neighbors, often reaching heights from 6 to 8 feet. Hellebore contains more than 200 different alkaloids, which are chemicals used to protect the plant from herbivores. All parts of the plant are highly toxic and can cause severe vomiting, low blood pressure, and even death. Nevertheless, the early colonists ground up the roots, mixed them with honey and flour, and used the mixture to kill rodents. Mothers dipped the family comb and hairbrush in the juice to kill lice. In the 1940s it was used as a treatment for high blood pressure, but its use was discontinued because of its adverse side effects.

FIGWORT

Scrophularia lanceolata
Bloom season: May–July
Figwort family (Scrophulariaceae)
Height: 3–8′

You have to get up close to see the small, unique flowers of figwort, but when you do, you are eye to eye with them—the plant can reach up to 8 feet tall. The oddly shaped flowers that somewhat resemble a camel's face are the color of brown figs, hence the name figwort, which means fig plant. In Shenandoah it can be found in Big Meadows and south into the Naked Creek Overlook area. Native Americans used the plant for many medicinal purposes. Women used it after childbirth to prevent cramps and bleeding. The leaves were also made into a poultice to calm the pain of sunburn or frostbite.

STINGING NETTLE

Urtica dioica
Bloom season: June–September
Nettle family (Urticaceae)
Height: 1–4′

Stinging nettle and its well-recognized friend poison ivy are two plants that those who love to be in the outdoors should get to know—at least from a distance. Every part of this plant and its relative, wood nettle (*Laportea canadensis*), are covered with tiny needles that produce an acute burning sensation when touched. Settlers knew that if they accidentally brushed up against nettle the crushed stems of jewelweed (*Impatiens sp.*) would help cool the burning sensation. Once cooked or dried, the leaves and stems lose their stinging properties. The young shoots and leaves of nettle can be cooked and eaten like spinach or made into a tea. Recent studies have shown that nettles may be helpful in decreasing inflammation associated with rheumatism.

HELLEBORINE

Epipactis helleborine

Bloom season: July–September

Orchid family (Orchidaceae)

Height: 1–3′

It is unheard of in the wildflower community to ever consider an orchid a weed, but there is one orchid that is fast acquiring this reputation. The helleborine orchid was introduced into New York from Europe in 1879 and within a century had spread to many states throughout the Northeast and Canada. Helleborine grows in almost any habitat but is usually found in partial shade. The tiny, usually green, flowers have a lavender tint, but there are many color variations, including white and yellow flowers. Some even have variegated leaves with white and cream markings. The plant has been found in the park along the Whiteoak Canyon Trail and in the Pocosin area.

Rose Twisted Stalk

PYGMY PIPES

Monotropsis odorata
Bloom season: March–April
Heath family (Ericaceae)
Height: 2–4"

An early-spring hike in Shenandoah National Park is often just what is needed after a long, cold winter. For those so inclined, unique flowers to seek out in the Sawmill Run area are pygmy pipes. Also known as sweet pinesap, the reddish-purple stems and flowers of pygmy pipes are often extremely camouflaged against the brown leaf litter and pine needles. You may actually be alerted by the plant's heady, spicy scent before you see it. The plant is saprophytic on the roots of trees, especially oaks. Rare throughout its range, pygmy pipes are found mostly in Virginia and North Carolina. It is either threatened or endangered in Florida, Kentucky, Maryland, and Tennessee. If you're fortunate enough to find this plant, please leave it for others to enjoy.

SPRING BEAUTY

Claytonia virginica
Bloom season: March–May
Montia family (Montiaceae)
Height: 6–12″

One of the earliest blooming wildflowers, spring beauty greets hikers along the Appalachian Trail with carpets of pinkish-white flowers striped with deeper shades of pink. The small corms (underground bulblike stems) of spring beauty were gathered by settlers in the spring, boiled, and eaten like potatoes. The corms were called "fairy spuds," because it took such a long time to collect enough for a meal. The plant was named for John Clayton, a botanist in the early 1700s who traveled throughout Virginia collecting and documenting plants.

RED TRILLIUM

Trillium erectum
Bloom season: April–June
Trillium family (Trilliaceae)
Height: 8–24"

One of only a handful of trillium species that occur in Shenandoah National Park, red trillium may also be called purple trillium and red-purple trillium. The imaginative folk name wake-robin refers to the return of migrant American robins to the area, which coincides with the bloom season. Its aroma will conjure up images of rotting meat from which the folk name stinking Benjamin is derived. "Benjamin" refers to a fragrance used in making incense. Native Americans used a poultice of the leaves to treat putrid ulcers, cancers, and gangrene. Uncommon in the park, this trillium can be found in the Swift Run Gap area and along the Appalachian Trail near Hightop summit.

ROSE TWISTED STALK

Streptopus lanceolatus
Bloom season: April–July
Lily family (Liliaceae)
Height: 12–32″

On an early-spring hike along Mill Prong Trail, wildflower enthu-
siasts are often pleasantly surprised to find the nodding rose-pink
flowers of rose twisted stalk. Also called rosy twisted stalk or
simply twisted stalk, it is an uncommon plant in the park found
in rich, moist woods. The zigzag pattern of the stem is usually
spotted first, as the tiny bell-shaped reddish-pink flowers hide
beneath the stem in a similar fashion to the flowers of Solomon's
seal (*Polygonatum biflorum*). Unlike the opposite leaves of Solomon's seal, the leaves are alternate in rose twisted stalk. Native
Americans steeped the root to treat eye infections such as sties.

TRUMPET HONEYSUCKLE

Lonicera sempervirens
Bloom season: April–September
Honeysuckle family (Caprifoliaceae)
Height: 3–20′

A high-climbing vine that can grow up to 20 feet in length, trumpet honeysuckle can be found in the park climbing up rock faces or trees in sunny areas. Sporting long, dazzling red tubular flowers, this is a favorite plant of ruby-throated hummingbirds, which enjoy the sweet nectar. The species name, *sempervirens,* means "evergreen," and the leaves remain throughout the winter. Native to the eastern United States, the plant is commonly called coral honeysuckle and is one of the food plants of spring azure butterfly caterpillars.

WILD COLUMBINE

Aquilegia canadensis
Bloom season: April–September
Buttercup family (Ranunculaceae)
Height: 6–30"

Decorating the Skyline Drive with bright splashes of red and yellow, wild columbine is a spectacular wildflower that blooms spring through summer. Found throughout the park, the plants often grow on rocky, wooded, or open slopes in bright sunlight. The showy nodding flower has 5 red, backward-pointing tubular petals that hang from slender, branching stems. Ruby-throated hummingbirds delve their long bills into the spurs to reach the sweet nectar reward and in doing so pick up a bit of pollen on their heads. Traveling to the next columbine, the feeding hummingbird brushes the pollen off its head onto the female part of the plant, thereby pollinating it.

ROSE AZALEA

Rhododendron prinophyllum
Bloom season: May–June
Heath family (Ericaceae)
Height: 6–12′

The first week in June is a marvelous time to be in Shenandoah National Park, as it typically begins the season of the rose azalea. In the central and southern sections of the park a spicy floral scent of cinnamon and cloves permeates the air from the rosy-pink flowers. This shrub is often mistaken for mountain laurel, but unlike the saucer-shaped flowers of mountain laurel, the pink flowers of rose azalea are funnel shaped. The flower stamens extend out beyond the petals, and each individual flower is much larger than the flower of mountain laurel. Many pollinators are attracted to the sweet fragrance of early azalea, which this shrub is sometimes called, including butterflies and ruby-throated hummingbirds.

PINK LADY'S SLIPPER

Cypripedium acaule
Bloom season: May–June
Orchid family (Orchidaceae)
Height: 6–15″

The distinctive flower of pink lady's slipper is composed of an inflated lower petal with reddish veins and a groove down the middle much like a moccasin, hence the alternate name, moccasin flower. The twisted, greenish-brown bracts (sepals) curve around the flower to help direct pollinating bees into the groove. Once inside the pouch, the bees must exit through small openings in the back of the flower to pick up pollen. Living a delicate symbiotic relationship with a very particular fungus, the plant takes more than ten years to produce a bloom. Take pleasure in these beautiful orchids, most commonly encountered in the southern section of Shenandoah, but please leave them for others to enjoy.

GAYWINGS

Polygala paucifolia
Bloom season: May–June
Milkwort family (Polygalaceae)
Height: 3–6"

A member of the milkwort family, gaywings, or fringed polygala, is by far the handsomest; its relatives tend to resemble the brushes used to clean baby bottles. Historically milkworts were used to help increase the amount of milk that mothers (and cows) could produce. Blooming in spring, the uncommon flowers occur in clusters that resemble flocks of whimsical magenta-colored cartoon butterflies. One petal is boat-shaped with a marvelous pink fringe frill at the end. Insects that land on the enticing fringed petal can pollinate the flower, but the flower also produces underground flowers that self-fertilize without opening.

DAME'S ROCKET

Hesperis matronalis
Bloom season: May–July
Mustard family (Brassicaceae)
Height: 1–3'

A showy plant with an unusual name, dame's rocket has large clusters of fragrant flowers with variable pink to white petals. A member of the large mustard family, it resembles a phlox except that it has 4 petals instead of the phlox's 5. Introduced from Eurasia in the 1600s as a fragrant garden flower, it is considered a nonnative invasive plant in Shenandoah National Park. It can be seen at Powell Gap and Gooney Run Overlook. The plant is a prolific seed producer and invades woodland edges and forests, taking over the habitat of native plants. The first part of the common name, "dame's," pertains to women and the Roman festival of matrons. "Rocket" is from a similar plant grown in the Mediterranean region called rocket, or arugula, which is used for salads.

PERFOLIATE HORSE GENTIAN

Triosteum perfoliatum
Bloom season: May–July
Honeysuckle family (Caprifoliaceae)
Height: 2–4′

Nestled at the base of the large leaves, the muted merlot-red flowers of perfoliate horse gentian are not obvious at first. The opposite leaves are fused together, surrounding the stem. Botanists called this phenomenon "perfoliate," as it appears that the stem perforates the leaves. In contrast, the bright orange berries of fall are quite conspicuous. Not a true gentian, the plant is a member of the honeysuckle family. The seeds were roasted as coffee, generating the common name wild coffee. The plant was used medicinally until the late 1800s as a purgative and to treat fevers, leading to its other common names, wild ipecac and fever root. This plant can be found at Naked Creek Overlook in the park.

MOUNTAIN LAUREL

Kalmia latifolia
Bloom season: May–July
Heath family (Ericaceae)
Height: 10–20′

Decorated with lustrous pink blossoms, mountain laurel bursts into full bloom during the month of June, creating a spectacular early-summer display. Virginians often abbreviate the name as simply laurel or ivy, as the bushy shrub forms dense, impenetrable thickets. The shrubs like to grow in openings in forested areas such as those found along the Limberlost Trail and the Appalachian Trail at Jenkins Gap. The saucer-shaped blossoms cover the shrub with striking clusters of pastel rose, pink, or white. The Civilian Conservation Corps (CCC) planted many of them while landscaping the Skyline Drive. The stamens are designed to spring like a bow and arrow when an insect trips the lever, plunking pollen on its back, ready to pollinate another flower.

TALL CORYDALIS

Capnoides sempervirens
Bloom season: May–September
Fumitory family (Fumariaceae)
Height: 1–3′

Tall corydalis is an audaciously colored wildflower with shouting hot-pink flowers and intense yellow lips. Pollinated by ants or wind, the delicate tubular flowers dangle on branched stems above divided pale bluish-green leaves. The seeds can live for many years in the soil and thrive in areas that have been burned. Sometimes called pink or pale corydalis, this plant can be found growing on rocky outcrops in such areas as Millers Head Trail near Skyland Resort in the central section of the park.

SPREADING DOGBANE

Apocynum androsaemifolium
Bloom season: June–July
Dogbane family (Apocynaceae)
Height: 1–4′

Very similar to its cousin, Indian hemp, spreading dogbane has nodding, pink bell-shaped flowers unlike the greenish-white upright flowers of Indian hemp. The stems and leaves have the consistency of rubber and when damaged exude a milky white juice called snake's milk, as it is very acrid. Dogbane was used by Cherokee Indians to bathe their dogs to treat mange. The sweet, lilac-scented flowers attract many potential pollinators, but only a few are able to get to the nectar reward. The flower acts as a natural flytrap, ensnaring smaller insects such as flies that cannot pull their tongues out of the cone-shaped, partially fused stamens that guard the nectar, saving it for more effective pollinators such as butterflies.

COMMON MILKWEED

Asclepias syriaca
Bloom season: June–August
Dogbane family (Apocynaceae)
Height: 3–5′

The name milkweed refers to the plant's milky-looking latex, which contains toxic chemicals to protect the plants from herbivores. Monarch butterflies are immune to these toxins and lay their eggs on the underside of milkweed leaves. When the larvae hatch, they eat the milkweed leaves and the bitter toxins accumulate in their bodies. The toxins act as a form of protection from predators. After one nibble, birds soon learn that monarchs taste bad and therefore do not eat them. Native Americans applied the latex to warts and ringworm. Stems were used to make cords and sewing thread. The tender young leaves, fruits, and flower buds were cooked and eaten. Great spangled fritillary shown here.

BOUNCING BET

Saponaria officinalis
Bloom season: June–September
Pink family (Caryophyllaceae)
Height: 16–32"

For most of the summer, bouncing bet, or soapwort, forms loose pink colonies along Skyline Drive. This ragtag flower stands as a reminder of one of the useful plants that early settlers brought with them from their gardens in Europe. Soapwort contains a substance known as saponin, which produces a soapy froth when agitated in water. The foam was not only used to clean hands and clothing but also added to flat beer to produce a nice frothy head. The phloxlike petals of this sweet-smelling flower are recurved, not unlike the hitched-up skirts of a washerwoman bending up and down over her washboard. Her name of course was Bet.

NODDING WILD ONION

Allium cernuum
Bloom season: July–August
Amaryllis family (Amaryllidaceae)
Height: 1–2'

Sleepy heads of nodding wild onion emerge in Big Meadows and along roadsides in midsummer. The tiny bell-shaped pinkish-lavender flowers hang in a cluster from the single drooping stem so that pollinators must hang upside down to reach the nectar. Like all onions, the stem and flower arise from an underground bulb, lending an onion flavor to the milk of cows that eat the leaves. The bulb was used in soups and to flavor meals. An onion poultice was made to place on the chest of children who were sick with a cough or the croup. The Algonquin name for this flower was *chigagou,* from which came the name for the city of Chicago.

JOE-PYE WEED

Eutrochium dubium
Bloom season: July–September
Aster family (Asteraceae)
Height: 2–6'

Sometimes people have such an influence on others that they are remembered long after their passing. Such is the case of an early New England herbalist named Joe Pye. His wide use of this plant to treat typhus, a bacterial disease carried by fleas and lice, so impressed his patients that they soon referred to the plant as Joe-Pye Weed. Native Americans used it as a diuretic and to soak inflamed joints. For good luck, the fuzzy head was kept in a pocket. The ground root in bathwater would soothe a fussy baby. Watch for these robust plants lining the Skyline Drive in late summer.

CARDINAL FLOWER

Lobelia cardinalis
Bloom season: July–September
Bellflower family (Campanulaceae)
Height: 2–5′

Unlike any other wildflower in the park, the intense scarlet color of cardinal flower commands attention—sometimes too much, as it is often the object of wildflower poachers in Shenandoah. The common name alludes to the bright red robes of Roman Catholic cardinals. The flower needs a consistently moist growing area and a pollinator. Most insects find the long tubular flowers too difficult to enter, but the long slender bills of hummingbirds are ideally suited to sip the nectar. Although the plant is fairly toxic, Native Americans added the chopped roots to food as a love potion.

TURTLEHEAD

Chelone glabra
Bloom season: July–September
Plantain family (Plantaginaceae)
Height: 1–3′

Turtlehead is known by an abundance of common names, including white turtlehead, balmony, snakehead, and fish mouth, which describe the unique shape of the flower, not its exquisite beauty. The Latin name comes from *chelone,* the Greek word for tortoise, referring to the shape of the flower, and *glabra,* meaning "smooth," describing the leaves and stem. Along with large bees that pollinate the flowers, territorial ruby-throated hummingbirds often vigorously defend these plants from other hummingbirds. Turtlehead is also the only food source for the larvae of the Baltimore checkerspot butterfly. Settlers to the area used the bitter leaves to reduce inflammation. They were also given to children to rid them of worms.

FALL PHLOX

Phlox paniculata
Bloom season: July–October
Phlox family (Polemoniaceae)
Height: 2–6′

Fragrant blooms of fall phlox sweeten the air as they sway on tall stems in late summer and early fall breezes. Also known as garden phlox, this plant is native to the eastern United States and Canada but has been extensively cultivated for many years as a fragrant, decorative addition to flower gardens. Butterflies such as swallowtails, fritillaries, and sulphurs are attracted to this plant and are often seen nectaring at the pink-hued flowers.

ALLEGHENY STONECROP

Hylotelephium telephioides
Bloom season: August–October
Stonecrop Family (Crassulaceae)
Height: 7–23″

Primarily found in the Central and Southern Appalachians, Allegheny stonecrop flowers in late summer and fall in Shenandoah. The name *telephioides* means "resembling Telephium," for Telephus, the son of Hercules. In true Herculean manner, this plant will withstand extreme conditions, as it is found on open rocky outcrops exposed to the elements. Its thick roots and succulent oval leaves store water to resist the drying effects of wind and sun. Sometimes called live-forever due to its hardiness, this and other plants that grow on rocky outcrops in the park are under pressure. Studies show that intense use of these areas by hikers and climbers has led to loss of plants at some popular cliff sites. Efforts are under way to preserve these special plant communities.

Greater purple fringed orchid

DWARF IRIS

Iris verna

Bloom season: March–May

Iris family (Iridaceae)

Height: 2–6″

Delightful showy clusters of dwarf iris entertain early-spring visitors to Shenandoah National Park. Unlike many irises, this small iris tends to grow in dry, sandy areas. You can see iris along the Appalachian Trail at Browns Gap near Milepost 83. If you look closely, you will notice 3 upright lavender petals bordered by 3 yellow-striped lavender sepals. The bright yellow lines help guide insects to the nectar. In Greek mythology, Iris was the goddess of the rainbow. Whenever a rainbow appeared, it meant that Iris was bringing a message from Olympus to someone on Earth.

ROUND-LOBED HEPATICA

Anemone americana
Bloom season: March–May
Buttercup family (Ranunculaceae)
Height: 4–6″

Contributing some of the first colors to the thawing earth in spring, the lovely pastel displays of hepatica paint the cool forests with delicate blooms. The plant sends up pink, blue, lavender, or white blossoms that stand on short stalks above the greenish-purple leaves. The rounded 3-lobed leaves give this plant the name hepatica. The word "hepatic" refers to the liver, and the leaves of this plant are indeed liver-shaped. Ancient physicians believed that plants that resembled human body parts had useful relevance to those parts. This belief, known as the Doctrine of Signatures, was widely followed for hundreds of years.

COMMON BLUE VIOLET

Viola sororia
Bloom season: March–June
Violet family (Violaceae)
Height: 3–8"

With the warm breath of spring, an assortment of violets can be found gracing the hiking paths in Shenandoah. Ranging in color from deep violet to yellow or white, 20 different species of violets grow in the park. Violets were valuable to the early colonists, as they are both medicinal and edible. The flowers could be made into jelly or candied in sugar as a sweet decoration for desserts. The leaves were used in salads or cooked as greens. The leaves contain salicylic acid, the main ingredient in aspirin, and were used to relieve headaches. Violets have long been a symbol of love, faithfulness, and good will. A cup of violet blossom tea is said to brighten up even a grouchy person.

VIRGINIA BLUEBELL

Mertensia virginica
Bloom season: April–May
Borage family (Boraginaceae)
Height: 1–2′

In early spring, nodding clusters of trumpet-shaped Virginia bluebells grow in moist, rich woods and along streams at low elevations. Also called Roanoke bells or Virginia cowslip, the flowers put on a spectacular show for hikers passing through a knee-high sea of pastel blue along trails such as the Dickey Ridge Trail. The young blossoms contain anthocyanin, which gives them a pinkish tinge. As the flowers develop, they increase in alkalinity, masking the red pigment, which makes the flowers turn blue to attract insects. Cowslip is the common name for a similar plant with yellow flowers native to Europe, which was rubbed on cows in the belief that it would protect them from the mischief of fairies.

MOSS PHLOX

Phlox subulata
Bloom season: April–May
Phlox family (Polemoniaceae)
Height: 2–8″

In Virginia the April sun warms cascades of moss phlox on gentle banks along the Skyline Drive. The miniature scene of pastel colors are formed from carpets of lavender, blue, and pink flowers that creep low to the rocky ground. The evergreen needle–like leaves are somewhat awl-shaped, which inspired the species name, *subulata*. Translated from Greek, the word *"phlox"* means "as a flame," referring to the colorful flowers. Bees, butterflies, and other early-spring flying insects visit the colorful flowers seeking a sip of sweet nectar.

WILD GERANIUM

Geranium maculatum
Bloom season: April–June
Geranium family (Geraniaceae)
Height: 8–20″

One of the most common trailside wildflowers in spring, wild geranium, or cranesbill, can be found throughout the park. Butterflies and bees visit the lilac-colored flowers, and white-tailed deer like to eat the blossoms. The seed case resembles a long stork or crane's bill. The Greek word for crane is *geranos,* which is the derivative of the generic name geranium. Wild geranium has many traditional Native American uses, including as treatment for diarrhea, thrush, and hemorrhoids. A poultice of chewed roots was used to treat the navel of a newborn baby.

SHOWY ORCHIS

Galearis spectabilis
Bloom season: April–June
Orchid family (Orchidaceae)
Height: 4–8″

The showy orchis is a member of the orchid family, one of the largest families of flowering plants in the world. Most orchids have evolved along with a specific pollinator. They exist in a codependent relationship with their pollinator, and orchids rely on a mutualistic relationship with a particular soil fungus that is found in close proximity to the roots. The delicate purple-and-white blooms of showy orchis grow best in slightly disturbed wooded areas and can be found along most trails in the park, especially in May. Please do not pick them, but do take a moment to appreciate the sweet scent of this spring beauty. You can find these pastel orchids along Fox Hollow Trail, in the north section of the park.

SPIDERWORT

Tradescantia virginiana
Bloom season: April–July
Spiderwort family (Commelinaceae)
Height: 5–15″

Native to eastern North America, the long grasslike leaves of spiderwort somewhat resemble a large green spider. The sap is stringy and mucuslike, undoubtedly the source of the common name cow slobber. The sap also somewhat resembles a sticky spiderweb material. Early herbalists looked for ways to recognize what ailments a particular plant could be used for, and most assumed that the plant would give clues as to its use. Under the Doctrine of Signatures, it was assumed that adding this plant to beer and drinking the mixture daily would be help treat spider bites. Recent studies have revealed that the blue stamens of spiderwort change to a pink color when exposed to radiation, creating a natural Geiger counter.

GILL-OVER-THE-GROUND

Glechoma hederacea

Bloom season: April–July

Mint family (Lamiaceae)

Height: 1–16″

Creeping along the ground in spring, gill-over-the-ground, or ground ivy, forms dense patches or carpet-like mats. The purple trumpet-shaped flowers bloom in moist woodlands, shaded places, and lawns throughout the park. The leaves are rounded or kidney shaped with scalloped edges. When stepped on they produce a pungent, earthy spice scent. The plant was used in Europe to ferment beer. Another common name is hedgemaids, and "gill" means "girl." Rich in vitamin C, the leaves were made into a tea and used as a spring tonic. It was also used for coughs and colds.

BLUETS

Houstonia caerulea
Bloom season: April–July
Madder family (Rubiaceae)
Height: 2–8"

Cheerful colonies of tiny pale-blue flowers pad open areas along trails and in picnic areas in the spring. The yellow bull's-eye center adds a spot of color between the 4 azure petals. Bluets are pollinated by bee flies, which have elongated mouthparts that form a long proboscis that they dip into the center to retrieve nectar. Bee flies hover in midair without resting on the flower, thus avoiding predators such as spiders and ambush bugs that often hide in wait to attack their victims. Bluets are also called Quaker ladies or Quaker bonnets in reference to an assembly of gray-blue bonnet–clad women.

WILD COMFREY

Cynoglossum virginianum
Bloom season: May–June
Borage family (Boraginaceae)
Height: 1–2′

In May or June you may also see the curled sky-blue flowers and large leaves of wild comfrey. This plant is similar in appearance to the common comfrey of Europe and Asia, and early settlers used it in a comparable manner, eating the leaves like cooked spinach. Unfortunately the plant contains toxins that may cause liver damage or cancer. Native Americans used the root to treat cloudy urine. They boiled the root in water and applied the medicine to itching private parts. They also drank it to improve memory.

APPALACHIAN BEARDTONGUE

Penstemon canescens
Bloom season: May–June
Plantain family (Plantaginaceae)
Height: 1–3′

The genus *Penstemon* has about 250 species in North America, with 4 species occurring in Shenandoah National Park. Frequently called gray beardtongue, Appalachian beardtongue is commonly found in the mountain areas, dry open banks, and parks of Virginia and the Appalachians. The Greek word *penstemon* means "5 stamens." They are often called beardtongues because of the small tuft of hairs on the sterile stamen. Native Americans used various species of penstemon to relieve toothaches.

PURPLE CLEMATIS

Clematis occidentalis
Bloom season: May–June
Buttercup family (Ranunculaceae)
Height: 3–6′

Purple clematis is an uncommon flower that finds refuge in the park. Blooming in spring, the trailing vines often climb over rocky and other undisturbed areas. These natives are so showy and exotic looking that many people think they are cultivated flowers. The genus name, *Clematis*, in Greek means "long, easily bent branches," and the species name, *occidentalis*, is Latin for "western." The plant produces 4 petal-like reddish-violet sepals that pale as they open into a pastel violet. The flower seeds that follow have long, silvery clusters of feathery plumes that can be carried in the wind.

BLUE-EYED GRASS

Sisyrinchium angustifolium
Bloom season: May–August
Iris family (Iridaceae)
Height: 6–20″

A bit like a treasure hunt, finding blue-eyed grass is sometimes not an easy task. Even though the plant has grasslike leaves, it is actually in the iris family, with the typical long parallel-veined leaves that help classify this family. The small blue flowers with yellow centers sit atop a flat stem and blend in with surrounding grass. Look for blue-eyed grass in Big Meadows in June through August.

HEAL ALL

Prunella vulgaris
Bloom season: May–September
Mint family (Lamiaceae)
Height: 3–12″

Heal all, or self-heal, is a low, creeping plant found along roadsides and trails. Introduced from Europe, this plant has been used
for many folk remedies. The plant has small flowers that surround
an elongated club-shaped head. Reminiscent of the shape of an
orchid, the pastel-purple flowers are hooded with a fringed lower
lip that is often pale purple to whitish in color. Traditionally a tea
was made from the leaves and used as a gargle for sore throats.
The tea was also used to treat fevers and diarrhea. Mixed with oil,
the crushed leaves were applied to the head for a headache.

TALL BELLFLOWER

Campanulastrum americanum
Bloom season: June–August
Bellflower family (Campanulaceae)
Height: 2–6′

Reaching up to 6 feet in height, tall bellflower is a bit of a misnomer, as the flowers are not bell shaped at all. The sky-blue 5-lobed flowers are flattened and resemble a pointed catcher's mitt rather than a bell. The long, curved style projects about an inch from the flower center, ensuring that pollinators such as bumblebees and butterflies are tagged with pollen when they come in for a sip of sweet nectar. The leaves and roots of tall bellflower were used in the treatment of severe coughs, including whooping cough and tuberculosis, or "consumption," as it was commonly called.

GREATER PURPLE FRINGED ORCHID

Platanthera grandiflora
Bloom season: June–August
Orchid family (Orchidaceae)
Height: 1–4'

One of the stars of the eastern flora, greater purple fringed orchid is found along a narrow band through the mid-eastern states. It is found only in a few counties in Virginia and at several locations in Shenandoah National Park. The plant is threatened, endangered, or extirpated in nearby states, and Shenandoah plays an important role in the efforts to preserve this rare beauty queen. The orchid lures in tiger swallowtails, skippers, and moths with sugar nectar. It then glues a pollen sac to their head for a ride to another flower for pollination.

PURPLE FLOWERING RASPBERRY

Rubus odoratus
Bloom season: June–August
Rose family (Rosaceae)
Height: 3–6′

The eye-catching magenta blooms of purple flowering raspberry can't be missed on a summer day along the Skyline Drive. A member of the rose family, this is the only species that does not have divided leaves. Instead the leaves are quite large, spreading up to 10 inches across, with a distinct maplelike shape. This thornless shrub can reach up to 6 feet high and typically grows in large stands in most open areas of the park. The stems are covered with sticky reddish hairs that help prevent small insects from crawling up to steal nectar. The tart, dry berries were gathered for use in pies and jellies or dried in the sun to save for winter use.

VIPER'S BUGLOSS

Echium vulgare

Bloom season: June–September

Borage family (Boraginaceae)

Height: 12–30"

Few members of the wildflower world can boast the brilliance of the blue flowers of viper's bugloss. A hardy introduction from Eurasia, the plant grows easily in disturbed areas and is commonly seen while traveling the Skyline Drive in summer. The leaves and stems are loaded with irksome hairs and spines, causing an irritation to the skin if touched. "Viper's" refers to the fruits, which have the shape of a snake's head. On sunny days the flowers are often loaded with cabbage white butterflies.

COMMON DAYFLOWER

Commelina communis
Bloom season: June–October
Spiderwort family (Commelinaceae)
Height: 4–14″

A favorite with children of all ages, common dayflower, or the Mickey Mouse flower, is a fun flower to spot in the park. Try looking for it at the south entrance near Waynesboro or in other open places throughout the park. Even though it appears to have 2 large bright-blue "ears," the third petal is very small and insignificantly translucent bluish-white, making it very difficult to distinguish. The blue flowers sparkle when the sun hits them due to clear cells in the petals. The flowers usually close by midday, so if you want to see this flower, begin your hunt early in the day.

WILD BERGAMOT

Monarda fistulosa
Bloom season: July–August
Mint family (Lamiaceae)
Height: 1.5–4′

Thriving in open areas along the Skyline Drive, the lilac-colored clusters of wild bergamot are one of the most common wildflowers of summer. The crushed leaves emit a pleasant citrusy-mint aroma apparently similar to the odor of oranges grown near Bergamo, Italy, hence the plant's name. The genus name, *Monarda,* was given to honor Nicholas Monardes, an early Spanish herbalist who in the 1500s was the first to write about the newly discovered American plants. The species name, *fistulosa,* means tube or pipelike, describing the long, curved flower parts. The leaves were widely used in folk medicine to treat respiratory disorders. Earl Grey tea relies on the essential oil from this flower for its distinctive flavor.

APPALACHIAN BELLFLOWER

Campanula divaricata
Bloom season: July–September
Bellflower family (Campanulaceae)
Height: 12–24″

Also known as southern harebell, the dainty blue bell-shaped flowers hang beneath spindly, branched stems often on rocky dry cliffs in Shenandoah. Other common names include small bonny bellflower, southern bellflower, and southern bluebell. The edges of the tiny flowers curl backward, exposing the long pistil. Native Americans steeped the roots in water and then drank the infusion to stop diarrhea. This plant essentially reaches its northern distribution in Shenandoah National Park. It is listed as an endangered species in the nearby state of Maryland.

APPALACHIAN IRONWEED

Vernonia glauca
Bloom season: July–October
Aster family (Asteraceae)
Height: 3–6′

Native to the eastern United States, Appalachian ironweed blooms in late summer and fall. The intense purple flowers are borne on tall stems that can reach up to 6 feet tall. Ironweed acquired its name from the tough fibrous stems that are difficult to break. The bright purple flowers are often accompanied by a splash of color from a multitude of colorful butterflies, including yellow tiger swallowtail butterflies, fritillaries, and migrating monarchs. Native Americans used the root as a tonic for women after childbirth. Ironweed is found throughout Shenandoah; look for stands near Beagle Gap in the southern section of the park.

INDIAN TOBACCO

Lobelia inflata

Bloom season: July–October

Bellflower family (Campanulaceae)

Height: 1–3′

A member of the bellflower family, Indian tobacco sports small lavender-colored flowers bracketed by a hairy stem and toothed oblong leaves. The plant grows in open woods and along the Skyline Drive. Native Americans smoked the dried leaves like tobacco as a treatment for asthma, but it also had many other uses as a medicinal plant. Toxic in high doses, this plant earned the common name of puke weed. A tea was made from this plant by Shenandoah herb doctors to remove toxins from the body.

GREAT BLUE LOBELIA

Lobelia siphilitica

Bloom season: August–September

Bellflower family (Campanulaceae)

Height: 2–4′

In autumn, moist areas along Skyline Drive and open streamsides in the park display scattered spikes of the true blue flowers of great blue lobelia, a member of the bellflower family. Even though all parts of the plant are poisonous, Native Americans have used it for an extensive list of medical treatments. At one time the plant was used as a treatment for venereal disease, hence the species name, *siphilitica*. An infusion of the roots or leaves was used to treat worms, colds, rheumatism, fevers, and other ailments. Used in place of marriage counseling, it was also believed that ingestion of the roots would heal an ailing marriage.

GRASS-LEAVED BLAZING STAR

Liatris pilosa
Bloom season: August–October
Aster family (Asteraceae)
Height: 1–3'

Liatris comprises one of the more attractive late-blooming wild-flower genera. The blazing stars are also commonly known as gay-feathers because of the lavender spikes of flowers that wave merrily like violet feathers in the late-summer sun. Along with several other species of blazing stars found in Shenandoah, the grass-leaved blazing star can be found along sandy road banks and trails, especially in the southern section of the park. Crimora Lake Overlook is a good place to spot these lovely flowers. Butterflies such as silvery spotted skippers find the flowers irresistible, so where you find these flowers blooming is also good butterfly habitat.

STIFF GENTIAN

Gentianella quinquefolia

Bloom season: August–October

Gentian family (Gentianaceae)

Height: 8–32″

A late bloomer, stiff gentian can be found amidst the goldenrods and asters of late summer. The tubular deep lilac–colored flowers are about 0.5 to 1 inch long in tight clusters atop a stem with 4 ridges. Found in rich moist woods, wet meadows, and slopes in eastern North America, this plant is threatened or endangered in many states. Another common name for this plant is ague weed, which refers to its use as a medicinal plant to reduce fevers. The word "ague" was a medical term used to describe fevers or chills. The name "gentian" was to honor King Gentius of Illyria, who lived more than 2,000 years ago. He was credited as being the first person to discover the medicinal value of a European gentian.

CLASPING HEART-LEAVED ASTER

Symphyotrichum undulatum

Bloom season: August–November

Aster family (Asteraceae)

Height: 1–4′

One fanciful story told by an early founder of the park was that Shenandoah means "Daughter of the Stars." The name is certainly fitting, as the meadows and waysides are filled with more than 15 species of starlike wildflowers known as asters. In fact, the word "aster" comes from the Greek word for star. One of the most common asters in the south section of the park is clasping heart-leaved aster, or as it is commonly called, wavy aster. The lavender-colored petals are not actually petals but florets that surround central disk flowers. Wavy aster is one of the food plants for the caterpillar of the pearl crescent butterfly.

A glowing field of
Golden Ragwort
in Big Meadows

HAIRY YELLOW FOREST VIOLET

Viola pubescens
Bloom season: March–May
Violet family (Violaceae)
Height: 6–16″

A common spring wildflower, hairy yellow forest violet, or downy yellow violet, can be found throughout the park in rich woods. Violets are either "stemless," with leaves and flowers arising on separate stalks, or "stemmed," with both the flowers and leaves arising from the stem. Hairy yellow forest violet is a stemmed violet with fine hairs on the stem and heart-shaped leaves. Smooth yellow forest violet (*V. pensylvanica*) is also found in the park. The flowers and leaves of violets were commonly used by settlers to make teas, salads, candies, wines, syrups, and jellies. They were also used medicinally as a cough syrup, a laxative, and as an external poultice for wounds. A common folk saying is that when the yellow violets bloom, it is time to start hunting for the delicious morel mushrooms.

COMMON DANDELION

Taraxacum officinale

Bloom season: March–October

Aster family (Asteraceae)

Height: 2–18″

One of the most widely recognized of all wildflowers, the common dandelion is also the most ignored and sometimes despised of all plants. Millions of dollars are spent each year to poison and kill this pugnacious plant. Considered a weed, the dandelion has evolved to be one of the most successful wildflowers ever known. After a long winter, settlers relished the fresh greens as a welcome and healthful addition to meals, used in salads or cooked. Dandelions boast more vitamin A than carrots. They also contain more vitamin C, iron, and calcium than spinach. The flower petals were traditionally made into a delicate wine. The serrated or toothed appearance of the leaves, which resemble a lion's teeth, gives rise to the plant's name—in French, *dent de lion.*

DYER'S WOAD

Isatis tinctoria
Bloom season: April–May
Mustard family (Brassicaceae)
Height: 1.5–4'

Dyer's woad, or woad, is easily confused with similar mustard plants that grow in open habitats. To identify dyer's woad, look closely on the leaves and stems for a whitish coating that comes off when rubbed. After the flowering period is over, black seeds hanging from the plant rattle in the breeze. Dyer's woad originated in Asia and was brought with early Virginia colonists as a source of blue dye called indigo blue. Indigotine, the chemical producing the blue dye, is found in the leaves and produced through fermentation. "Woad" refers to the area in France where the plant was cultivated; *tinctoria* means "used in dyeing."

PERFOLIATE BELLWORT

Uvularia perfoliata
Bloom season: April–May
Meadow Saffron family (Colchicaceae)
Height: 6–18″

Along lush trails throughout Shenandoah, the melodious song of the wood thrush and the pale yellow nodding flowers of bellwort welcome spring hikers. The thin bell-shaped flowers were thought to resemble the uvula that hangs down from the soft palate in the throat, hence the genus name, *Uvularia*. The ending "wort" usually signifies that the plant was used for medicinal purposes. A tea made from the plant to relieve sore throats. The young, tender stems were eaten like asparagus. Iroquois not only ate the roots, or rhizomes, but also used them to heal wounds, and a poultice was made to treat boils. Other common species of bellwort found in Shenandoah include mountain bellwort (*U. puberula*) and sessile bellwort (*U. sessilifolia*).

YELLOW LADY'S SLIPPER

Cypripedium parviflorum
Bloom season: April–May
Orchid family (Orchidaceae)
Height: 8–12″

The lady's slipper, or moccasin flower, is one of more than 30 orchid species recorded within the boundaries of Shenandoah National Park. Lady's slippers have a balloonlike pouch that resembles a bedroom slipper. The veins in the leaves resemble nerves, and these flowers were sometimes called nerve roots. Used to treat nervous system disorders, the powdered root was steeped in boiling water and used as a tranquilizing tonic. Also called American valerian, they were considered to have similar sedative properties as European valerian. Large yellow lady's slippers are found in rich woods; the less-common, small variety grows in moist areas.

EARLY MEADOW RUE

Thalictrum dioicum
Bloom season: April–May
Buttercup family (Ranunculaceae)
Height: 1–2'

Blooming in April, early meadow rue is a 1- to 2-foot-tall graceful plant found in moist, open woods. Other meadow rues, such as tall meadow rue (*T. polygamum*) and skunk meadow rue (*T. revolutum*), bloom later in the summer. The gray-green foliage is made up of many small, round, scalloped leaflets on long stalks. Yellowish-green flowers hang in small fringed tassels that are sometimes tinted purple. Native Americans used the root of this plant to treat vomiting, diarrhea, and heart palpitations.

GOLDEN ALEXANDERS

Zizia aurea
Bloom season: April–June
Carrot family (Apiaceae)
Height: 1–3′

The many clustered flowers of golden Alexanders somewhat resemble a flat-topped yellow broccoli head called an umbel, for an umbrella-like inflorescence. The larvae of black swallowtail butterflies munch on its sharp-pointed leaves and flowers. The name golden Alexanders denotes the golden age of Alexander the Great. The genus, *Zizia*, was named for a German botanist by the name of Johan Baptist Ziz. The species name, *aurea*, comes from the Latin word meaning "golden yellow." Golden Alexanders is often confused with several other similar flowers, including heart-leaved golden Alexanders (*Z. aptera*), which has heart-shaped basal leaves; yellow pimpernel (*Taenidia integerrima*), which has untoothed leaflets; and bearded meadow-parsnip (*Thaspium barbinode*), which has hairy stem joints. It blooms in late spring.

WOOD BETONY

Pedicularis canadensis
Bloom season: April–June
Broomrape family (Orobanchaceae)
Height: 5–14″

The many-hued flowers of wood betony encircle thick spikelike stems with colors ranging from yellow to reddish to purple or a combination of all three. The plant is often called lousewort from the belief that lice were transferred from the flowers to grazing cattle. In addition, the flowers look very much like the hooked claws of a louse. Native Americans cooked the spring leaves as food. The chopped root was added to food as a love charm. You can see this flower at Meadow Spring parking area and throughout the park.

MARSH MARIGOLD

Caltha palustris
Bloom season: April–June
Buttercup family (Ranunculaceae)
Height: 8–24″

Resembling a large buttercup, marsh marigold has 5 to 9 deep-yellow glossy petal-like sepals. The stem is hollow and the glossy leaves are rounded or kidney shaped. This spring bloomer grows in wet areas and can be seen in many seepage areas in the park, including Big Meadows Campground, Lands Run Falls, Nicholson Hollow, and the Naked Creek area. The toxic juice the plant contains was used to remove warts and as a rheumatism treatment. In spring, settlers gathered the leaves to cook and, after repeatedly changing the water, ate it like spinach. Prepared in a similar manner, the flower buds were cooked, pickled, or made into wine and were used to give homemade butter a nice golden color.

GOLDEN RAGWORT

Packera aurea
Bloom season: April–July
Aster family (Asteraceae)
Height: 1–3'

Golden ragwort is also known as golden groundsel, heart-leaved groundsel, and butterweed. The plants are hairy when young but then lose their hairs. The bottom, or basal, leaves are heart shaped; the upper leaves are bluntly toothed. Found in Big Meadows, the small yellow flowers attract bees and butterflies. The plant may cause skin irritation if touched. Native Americans used golden ragwort for a wide variety of medicinal purposes. A preparation of the flowers was given to children to reduce fevers and was widely used for women's problems and to speed childbirth. It was also used for heart problems and for broken bones. The plant contains toxic alkaloids that have been shown to cause cancer.

INDIAN CUCUMBER ROOT

Medeola virginiana
Bloom season: May–June
Lily family (Liliaceae)
Height: 1–3'

Native to eastern North America, Indian cucumber root is found scattered in rich woods throughout the park. The whorled leaves are in 2 tiers, with small greenish-yellow flowers hiding beneath the top tier. As clearly suggested by the name, Native Americans ate the root of this plant just as we would a cucumber. The root, or rhizome, has the consistency of a radish but tastes like a cucumber. The chewed root was also placed on fishhooks as bait. In late summer, dark bluish-purple berries form and the upper whorl of leaves turns red to attract animals such as birds to spread the seeds. Look for this plant along Gravel Springs Trail.

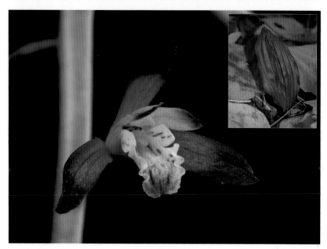

PUTTYROOT

Aplectrum hyemale
Bloom season: May–June
Orchid family (Orchidaceae)
Height: 10–16″

Quite a lonely flower, puttyroot orchid is in the genus *Aplectrum,* of which the only other member lives in Japan. The yellowish-brown flower has been described as sallow or dingy, but if you look closely, it is quite a beauty. The fringed white petals have maroon stippling; the lateral petals are green and brown. The inch-thick root, or corm, is attached to the next one by a slender stalk, generating the plant's other common name of Adam and Eve, as they walk hand in hand. *Aplectrum* means "without spurs," which many orchids possess to deliver nectar. *Hyemale* means "winter" and refers to the single leaf that remains throughout the winter until the next flower appears in spring. Native Americans and early settlers used the sticky root as putty to mend broken pottery.

SQUAWROOT

Conopholis americana
Bloom season: May–June
Broomrape family (Orobanchaceae)
Height: 2–8″

Hikers in rich woods throughout the park may take a second look after spotting what appears to be a brownish-yellow fleshy pinecone. On closer inspection, they'll find this odd-looking wildflower. It does not produce chlorophyll and never turns green. Squawroot does have scaly leaflike appendages, but it derives all its needed nutrients from the roots of trees, especially oaks. The plant was collected by Native Americans to treat wounds. Perhaps described best by another common name, bear corn, this flower is a favorite food of bears. In Shenandoah, it may represent up to 40 percent of their annual diet.

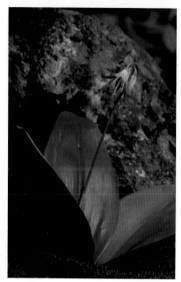

BLUEBEAD LILY

Clintonia borealis
Bloom season: May–July
Lily family (Liliaceae)
Height: 6–16″

Bluebead lily blooms at high altitude on Hawksbill Mountain in Shenandoah. Also called yellow Clintonia or simply Clintonia, the plant is a member of the lily family characterized by wide leaves with parallel veins. *Clintonia* honors the governor of New York from 1769 to 1828, DeWitt Clinton; *borealis* reflects that it is considered a northern inhabitant. The common name bluebead comes from the midnight-blue rounded berries that replace the 6-petaled yellowish-green flowers in the fall. Very slow growing, it may take 10 to 12 years for this plant to flower. Using only their teeth, Native Americans tapped decorative patterns into the broad leaves.

BUTTERFLY WEED

Asclepias tuberosa

Bloom season: June–August

Dogbane family (Apocynaceae)

Height: 1–2′

In summer, open areas along the Skyline Drive are often sprinkled with clusters of brilliant orange flowers. Butterfly weed, or butterfly milkweed, is a nectar source for many butterflies, including monarchs, swallowtails, and fritillaries. The genus name, *Asclepias,* honors Asclepius, the Greek god of healing. It is sometimes called pleurisy root, as Native Americans used the root as a cure for pleurisy and other lung ailments. Recently scientists have found that it contains a cardiac glycoside, a chemical that affects the heart and other body systems. This is the active ingredient in some heart medications but can be poisonous in large doses.

COMMON ST. JOHN'S WORT

Hypericum perforatum
Bloom season: June–September
St. John's wort family (Hypericaceae)
Height: 12–30"

Named for St. John the Baptist, the bright-yellow starry flowers of St. John's wort have been used for centuries to ward off evil spirits and as a charm against witchcraft. The plant has been used for many medicinal purposes, including treating wounds, insect bites, tuberculosis, and other respiratory problems. It also has a long history for use in treating mental disorders and nerve pain. There is some scientific evidence that St. John's wort may be useful for mild depression, but clinical trials have shown that it is no more effective than a placebo for more severe depression. As with any medication, consult a physician before taking herbals. St. John's wort can cause sun sensitivity, and it interacts with many important medications, such as birth control pills, antidepressants, heart medications, anticoagulants, and cancer medications.

COMMON MULLEIN

Verbascum thapsus

Bloom season: June–September

Figwort family (Scrophulariaceae)

Height: 2–8′

Brought to North America from Europe, common mullein's large, woolly leaves have a rough flannel-like texture and were used as warm padding for shoes in winter, as a poultice for rheumatism, and even as toilet paper. Tea made from the plant was used as a cough remedy for asthma and whooping cough. Leaves and stalks were used to make a purple-brown dye for clothing, and the stalks were dipped in tallow and used as torches. The seeds, which contain the toxin rotenone, were used by Native Americans to paralyze fish for easy catching. Rotenone is routinely used in organic farming as a pesticide but recently has been linked with Parkinson's disease–like symptoms. The smaller, related moth mullein (*V. blattaria*) has white or pale yellow flowers and less-prominent leaves.

BLACK-EYED SUSAN

Rudbeckia hirta
Bloom season: June–October
Aster family (Asteraceae)
Height: 1–3′

The bright color and hardiness of the black-eyed Susan make it a favorite of wildflower lovers. Thriving in poor soil, black-eyed Susan is a hardy plant that can withstand drought and long days in the sun. Carolus Linnaeus, considered to be the father of scientific classification, named the genus *Rudbeckia* to honor a Swedish botanist, Olaus Rudbeck. The bright-yellow "petals" are actually sterile ray flowers designed to attract a wide variety of pollinators. The actual fertile flowers make up the black or dark-brown eye. Look closely at the center, and you may see a ring of yellow blossoms showing the yellow pollen. Look for this recognizable flower in open areas of the park such as the Beagle Gap area.

BUTTER-AND-EGGS

Linaria vulgaris
Bloom season: June–October
Plantain family (Plantaginaceae)
Height: 1–4′

Filling Big Meadows with soft golden-haired colonies, a colorful flower called butter-and-eggs helps to usher in the earthy hues of fall; the blooms often last until the first frosts. The delightfully descriptive common name was given for the duet of colors displayed by the flower, pale yellow for the butter and yellowish-orange for the eggs. Introduced from Europe, the plant has spread across North America and in some western states is considered a noxious weed. Another common name is toadflax, as the leaves are similar to those of flax and the flower can be pressed to imitate the open and closing mouth of a croaking frog.

TURK'S CAP LILY

Lilium superbum
Bloom season: July–August
Lily family (Liliaceae)
Height: 3–8′

As the warm days of summer settle in, the bright-orange splashes of colorful Turk's cap lilies delight travelers along the Skyline Drive. The common name Turk's cap comes from the flower's similarity to a colorful traditional Turkish felt hat with recurved brim and pointed top. Large yellow tiger swallowtail butterflies can often be seen nectaring at these lilies. When visiting a flower, they are dusted on their wings and backs with rusty brown pollen from the prominent stamens before they fly off to the next lily and deposit the pollen, completing the cycle. Native Americans used the starchy dried bulb of lilies as a thickening agent for soup.

CANADA GOLDENROD

Solidago canadensis

Bloom season: July–September

Aster family (Asteraceae)

Height: 1–6′

Falsely accused of causing allergies, the golden, wandlike flowers of goldenrod that wave gracefully in late-summer breezes do not cause hay fever at all. The pollen is actually quite heavy and thick and cannot be carried on the wind. It blooms at the same time as ragweed, which does indeed cause many allergy sufferers to sniffle and sneeze. Known as "Liberty Tea," goldenrod was used as an alternative for imported tea after the Boston Tea Party. In 1918 goldenrod was recommended as the national flower of the United States, but in 1986 it lost to the rose. There are more than 20 species of goldenrod found in Shenandoah National Park. Cliffs in the park are wonderful for views, but be careful not to step on Rand's goldenrod (*S. randii*), which is rare in Virginia.

SPOTTED JEWELWEED

Impatiens capensis
Bloom season: July–September
Touch-me-not family (Balsaminaceae)
Height: 2–5′

The dog days of summer are brightened by large stands of sparkling orange jewelweed flowers. The 2- to 5-foot-tall stems wave toward cars passing by on the Skyline Drive. Common in wet areas, this flower blooms when hummingbird migration is peaking. If you are a quiet observer, you can often see ruby-throated hummingbirds drinking thirstily from the flowers. Another name for this plant is spotted touch-me-not, as the slightest touch will make the mature seedpods pop, flinging the seeds up to 5 feet away. Sap from the stems and leaves has long been a folk treatment to calm the itch from poison ivy and stinging nettles.

WOODLAND SUNFLOWER

Helianthus divaricatus
Bloom season: July–October
Aster family (Asteraceae)
Height: 2–7′

Native to eastern North America, the woodland sunflower is found in open areas of the park and is commonly seen along the Skyline Drive in late summer. Sometimes called rough sunflower, the stem is smooth, but the leaves are rough on the top and hairy below. Sunflowers were used by Native Americans to make purple, blue, and yellow dyes for clothing and basket fibers. Sunflowers were also used to treat sores as well as snake and spider bites. To keep from overheating, the mature flower heads always face east, although the immature buds track the movement of the sun across the horizon. Goldfinches and many other birds love the nutritious seeds. Sunflower seeds are high in folate, which is a B vitamin women need to prevent birth defects in their children.

CROWNBEARD

Verbesina occidentalis
Bloom season: August–October
Aster family (Asteraceae)
Height: 3–6'

Crownbeard commonly forms large golden colonies of tall summer flowers in open fields and meadows in the park. Crownbeard is very similar in shape and appearance to wingstem (*V. alternifolia*), but the leaves are opposite instead of the alternate leaves of wingstem. Also called yellow crownbeard or stickweed, the 2 to 8 yellow ray flowers droop around the central cone of each flower. The opposite leaves are coarse and sandpapery, tapering at both ends. Like its look-alike, wingstem, distinctive "wings" run the length of the stem.

A male Devil's bit flower graces Big Meadows

DUTCHMAN'S BREECHES

Dicentra cucullaria
Bloom season: March–April
Fumitory family (Fumariaceae)
Height: 4–12"

In spring, the billowy white blooms of Dutchman's breeches resemble a clothesline full of puffy pantaloons. The nodding flowers have 2 plump legs tipped with a lacy yellow waistband. Attached to the flower seeds is a fleshy food patch rich in fats and proteins called an elaiosome. Elaios means "oil," and som means "body." Ants carry the seed back to their underground home, where they eat the nutritious elaiosome and discard the seed as trash. This symbiotic process provides a means for the seeds to spread and germinate. You can find Dutchman's breeches along trails in rich forests throughout the park, including Dickey Ridge Trail.

BLOODROOT

Sanguinaria canadensis
Bloom season: March–April
Poppy family (Papaveraceae)
Height: 2–6"

Found throughout the park in rich, moist forests, bloodroot is one of the earliest of the woodland wildflowers to emerge in spring. With crisp white daisylike petals, these plants often form large colonies on the forest floor. The delicate flowers last only a few days. Ants spread the seeds, and the single wavy-lobed leaf remains into the spring. The stem and roots contain a thick red-orange sap, inspiring the Latin name, *Sanguinaria,* which means "blood red." The sap was used to dye wool an orange color, and Native Americans used it as a dye for skin paint and clothing. A common name is puccoon, from an Indian word for "red."

TRAILING ARBUTUS

Epigaea repens
Bloom season: March–May
Heath family (Ericaceae)
Height: 1–2″

A true harbinger of spring, trailing arbutus can be found in the south section of the park along trails in sandy or rocky woodland areas with dry acidic soil. Blooming in mid-March, the plant is sometimes called mayflower, as it was supposedly the first flower the Pilgrims saw after their first winter in the New World. Another common name is gravel plant, as the leaves were used to cure "gravel," or kidney stones. The oval evergreen leaves have a leathery texture, and the woody stems are covered with reddish hairs. Flowers are white, turning pink quickly and then browning as they age. The flowers have a fresh, alluring perfume similar to that of Ivory Snow laundry detergent. The flowers were used to make spring wreaths and to fill baskets to celebrate spring.

SQUIRREL CORN

Dicentra canadensis
Bloom season: March–May
Fumitory family (Fumariaceae)
Height: 4–12″

Often confused with the similar Dutchman's breeches, squirrel corn does not have the tiny inverted leggings. Instead this early-spring bloomer is heart shaped. A more appropriate name for this flower might be "white valentine," as the flowers resemble puffy marshmallow hearts. Other common names include turkey corn and bleeding heart. Often used as a love charm, the adorable flowers of squirrel corn audaciously display their message of love above a lacy cover of leaves. The roots contain inflated yellowish nodules that store nutrients for the plant. The nodules, which somewhat resemble corn kernels, are eaten by squirrels, chipmunks, mice, and wild turkeys.

RUE ANEMONE

Thalictrum thalictroides
Bloom season: March–May
Buttercup family (Ranunculaceae)
Height: 4–8″

The thin, flexible stems of rue anemone, commonly called wind-flower, are well suited to handle the shifting winds of early spring in Shenandoah. Often found growing in the same habitat as wood anemone, the white flowers of rue anemone are very similar in appearance. Both plants have flowers with white sepals that look like petals, but rue anemone has 2 to 3 flowers as opposed to the single flower of wood anemone. The rounded leaves of rue anem-one also help to separate it from wood anemone, which has pointed leaves. The flowers are sometimes visited by early-season insects, but they rely mostly on wind pollination. To keep the pollen dry, the flowers close at night as well as times when dew or rain might moisten the pollen and make it too heavy to float on the winds.

CUT-LEAVED TOOTHWORT

Cardamine concatenata
Bloom season: March–June
Mustard family (Brassicaceae)
Height: 8-10″

Blooming in early spring, cut-leaved toothwort sports a delicate cluster of small, 4-petaled, white, bell-shaped flowers that often blush with pastel pink highlights. The deeply cut toothed leaves form whorls of 3 around the stem. The toothlike projections along the root prompted early physicians to use the powdered root to cure toothaches. The leaves were eaten as a spring herb, and the root was used like pepper. This is the primary food plant of the West Virginia white butterfly caterpillar in Shenandoah. The caterpillars will not survive if they try to feed on the similar-looking introduced alien garlic mustard. Cut-leaved toothwort is found throughout the park in rich woods, especially in low to mid-elevations.

SHALE BARREN PUSSYTOES

Antennaria virginica

Bloom season: April–May

Aster family (Asteraceae)

Height: 4–16″

Found in dense silvery colonies, pussytoes are in the same family as their field mates, daisies and dandelions. The stubby white flower heads, which resemble kittens' toes, are tiny soft-haired individual flowers bound tightly together. The female flowers are taller and fuzzier than the males. Bees and other small flying insects transfer the pollen from male flowers to female flowers. To prevent robbers such as ants that would steal the nectar without pollinating, the plant has fuzzy stems to catch the would-be thieves. Shale barren pussytoes is endemic to a small area of the Appalachians, including Shenandoah National Park. At least 3 other species of pussytoes can be found in dry, open areas of the park.

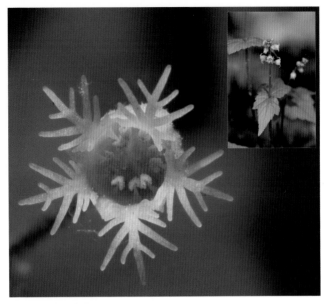

MITERWORT

Mitella diphylla
Bloom season: April–May
Saxifrage family (Saxifragaceae)
Height: 10–18″

A masterpiece in miniature, the delicate lacy flowers of miterwort are one of nature's most spectacular handiworks. Hike the Milam Gap Trail in spring to admire this incredibly delicate plant growing in the moist boggy areas near the Rapidan River crossing. Each white flower is less than 0.25 inch across and is best viewed with a magnifying lens or close-up camera lens. You can also look through the wrong end of a pair of binoculars, which will act like a magnifying glass. The genus name, *Mitella,* refers to the shape of the seed capsules, which resemble a bishop's hat, or miter.

LARGE-FLOWERED TRILLIUM

Trillium grandiflorum
Bloom season: April–May
Trillium family (Trilliaceae)
Height: 8–18″

The logo of the Shenandoah National Park Association, the large-flowered trillium has striking 3-inch white flowers. The showy foliage and floral parts of trillium are counted in multiples of 3, with 3 petals, 3 sepals, and 3 leaves. The white flower petals gradually fade into a subtle pastel pink color, often with maroon streaks. Attached to a trillium seed is a nutritious food particle that ants carry home with them, dispersing the seeds in a symbiotic relationship. Large colonies of trilliums can be found in the central section of the park at Swift Run Gap and the Lewis Mountain area.

SWEET WHITE VIOLET

Viola blanda
Bloom season: April–May
Violet family (Violaceae)
Height: 1–5″

At least 5 species of white violets are found in the park, often growing in different habitats. Sweet white violet (*Viola blanda*) and Canada violet (*V. canadensis*) are common in the park and can be found growing in rich, moist woods. Sweet white violet is fragrant with petals that reflex backward like a dog's ears. The white petals of Canada violet have purple backsides and yellow throats. Creamy violet (*V. striata*) likes to grow in disturbed areas and is often found near old home sites. Wild white violet (*V. macloskeyi* ssp. *pallens*) can be found growing in wet seepage areas.

WOOD ANEMONE

Anemone quinquefolia
Bloom season: April–June
Buttercup family (Ranunculaceae)
Height: 4–8″

Early spring gently awakens the brown leaf-covered earth with a lovely display of tender wildflowers. One of these early-spring bloomers, wood anemone is frequently found along trails in the park, including the Appalachian Trail. The 5 delicate, bright white petals of wood anemone are not petals at all but sepals that look like petals. The dark green leaves are very deeply cut, which makes them appear to be leaflets. "Anemone" comes from the Anemoi, who were the Greek wind gods. The name is quite fitting, as these flowers bloom with the warm spring winds.

BLADDER CAMPION

Silene vulgaris
Bloom season: April–August
Pink family (Caryophyllaceae)
Height: 6–24″

The unusual inflated flowers of bladder campion are eye-catching and quite attractive, although this introduced plant is considered a weed in most areas. This plant is widespread in the park, and at many overlooks you can see the curious white flowers that look a bit like a tiny squeaky toy made from paper. The inflated part is made up of 5 fused sepals with an intricate network of pink veins. The 5 white petals are deeply lobed with 10 long, thin, protruding stamens. Probably introduced from Europe to the United States as a food source, the leaves are commonly cooked and eaten in the Mediterranean region. Bladder campion is one of only a few plants capable of growing on metal-contaminated soils, and these properties are undergoing scientific studies.

SWEET CICELY

Osmorhiza claytonii
Bloom season: May–June
Carrot family (Apiaceae)
Height: 16–32″

To add flavor to their cooking pots, early settlers used the aromatic leaves and roots of sweet cicely. Small, inconspicuous white flowers top stems reaching above the fernlike leaves that are bluntly toothed and divided into 3. Native Americans ground the root to use for coughs and sore throats. They also used it for eyewash, as the constant exposure to campfires and smoke often irritated their eyes. The flower is found in most areas of the park in rich woods, and you can see it along the Story of the Forest Trail at Big Meadows. A similar plant, anise root (*O. longistylis*), boasts roots that have an anise or licorice taste and odor.

MAYAPPLE

Podophyllum peltatum
Bloom season: May–June
Barberry family (Berberidaceae)
Height: 12–18″

Hiding below 2 round-lobed leaves the size of a dinner plate, the nodding white flower of mayapple dangles between the branching stems. In early spring, large patches of mayapple bloom in rich woods throughout the park. The broad leaves gather energy from sunlight before the leaves of woodland trees are fully developed and shade the forest floor. Also known as American mandrake, all parts of the plant are poisonous except the ripe fruit, which was eaten or made into a lemonade-like drink. Native Americans used the plant to treat warts and cancers. A toxin found in the rhizome of the plant is used in cancer treatments.

WHITE BANEBERRY

Actaea pachypoda
Bloom season: May–June
Buttercup family (Ranunculaceae)
Height: 16–32″

In spring, the feathery white flower clusters of white baneberry bloom in rich woods in Shenandoah. The delicate flowers often go unnoticed, but in summer the berries are quite distinctive and often stop curious hikers for a closer look. Attached to the bright-red stalk, the pea-size white berries sport a distinctive dark-blackish dot formed by the remaining end of the stigma, which is a part of a plant's female reproductive structure. The berries resemble the porcelain eyes that were placed in china dolls in the 1800s, promoting the common name for this plant, doll's eyes. The name baneberry comes from the toxicity of the berries, which can cause severe diarrhea, dizziness, and hallucinations.

WILD SARSAPARILLA

Aralia nudicaulis
Bloom season: May–July
Ginseng family (Araliaceae)
Height: 6–15″

Along the Snead Farm Loop Trail, you may find patches of wild sarsaparilla growing in semi-open wooded areas. In spring the flowers can be found under the large leaves with 3 to 5 oval, toothed leaflets. The greenish-white flowers form a 1- to 2-inch-round cluster like small golf balls, which are replaced by dark blue-black berries in late summer. The berries were used to make a wine similar in taste to elderberry wine and are relished by wildlife. Seeds that have passed through a bear's digestive system have about a 75 percent higher germination rate than uneaten seeds. Native Americans made a poultice for wounds by chewing the roots and leaves.

DEVIL'S BIT

Chamaelirium luteum
Bloom season: May–July
Swamp-pink family (Heloniadaceae)
Height: 1–4'

If there was ever a flower that was misnamed, it might be this one. Devil's bit is a common name given to another plant in Europe called devil's-bit scabious, whose root appeared to be bitten off by the Devil. The genus name, *Chamaelirium*, means "ground lily," although it is neither a lily nor does it lie on the ground. The species name, *luteum*, means "yellow," but the flower is white, although it does turn yellowish when dried. A more pleasing and perhaps more appropriate name is fairywand, as the long, gracefully arching flowers of the male plant resemble a wand. The flowers of the female plant are in dense terminal spikes. The plant can be seen in Big Meadows, but take care not to damage this park rarity.

WHITE CLINTONIA

Clintonia umbellulata
Bloom season: May–July
Lily family (Liliaceae)
Height: 8–24"

This striking member of the lily family can be found in Shenandoah along trails that pass through rich cove hardwood forests. Native to eastern North America, this plant is only found from the tip of western New York to northern Georgia. Also known as speckled wood lily or white bluebead lily, its closest relative in the park, bluebead lily (*C. borealis*), is found only on high-altitude peaks in Shenandoah. The small white flowers that sit atop a thin, downy stalk are often speckled with green and purple spots.

BOWMAN'S ROOT

Gillenia trifoliata

Bloom season: May–July

Rose family (Rosaceae)

Height: 1–3′

Early colonists believed that purging was often a cure for illness, and many plants were used for such purposes, including Bowman's root. Sometimes called American ipecac, as it was used as an emetic, the powdered root was given to the patient until he vomited. Native Americans also used the root in the same purgative manner, hence another common name, Indian physic. Bowman's root can be found growing in sunny areas in Shenandoah, especially on open slopes along the Skyline Drive and beside the stone walls at the park's many overlooks.

GOAT'S BEARD

Aruncus dioicus
Bloom season: May–July
Rose family (Rosaceae)
Height: 3–6'

Growing along shade-dappled banks at the edges of rich woods in Shenandoah, the tall waving clusters of creamy-white goat's beard flowers decorate the waysides in early summer. Common along Skyline Drive, you can see these lovely flowers, which resemble the beard of a billy goat, near Marys Rock Tunnel. Another common name for goat's beard is bride's feathers, which refers to the early-summer bloom time of June. Expensive ostrich feathers were commonly used as decorations in weddings, but the lacy white blooms of bride's feathers could be used as a substitute adornment, especially the elaborate male flowers.

FALSE SOLOMON'S SEAL

Maianthemum racemosum
Bloom season: May–July
Ruscus family (Ruscaceae)
Height: 16–32"

Although the plant is sometimes confused with Solomon's seal, the flowers of false Solomon's seal are the clue to proper identification. Both plants have alternate leaves on a long, gracefully arching stem, but unlike the duet of greenish flowers that dangle beneath Solomon's seal, the creamy white flowers of false Solomon's seal grace the tip of the slightly zigzagged stem. Bees visit the sweet-smelling flowers. In fall, wild birds and small mammals pluck the red berries that replace the flowers. The seeds pass through the digestive system of the birds and animals, helping spread the seeds throughout the forest.

QUEEN ANNE'S LACE

Daucus carota

Bloom season: May–October

Carrot family (Apiaceae)

Height: 2–3′

Widespread across North America and one of the most well known of all wildflowers, Queen Anne's lace was introduced from Europe. Also called wild carrot, the flat, lacy-patterned cluster of white flowers and finely dissected leaves can take over fields and roadsides. To make a colorful bouquet, children placed the stems of the white flowers in jars of vegetable dye and the next day awoke to a rainbow of colors. Farmers disliked the plant, as it imparted a bitter taste to milk when their cows ate it. As a folk remedy to avoid pregnancy, the seeds were finely crushed and then taken with a glass of water as a morning-after contraceptive. In the Shenandoah Valley, a tea was made from the plant to relieve backache.

RAMPS

Allium tricoccum
Bloom season: June–July
Amaryllis family (Amaryllidaceae)
Height: 6–20″

The 2 or 3 straplike onion-scented leaves of ramps, or wild leeks, emerge in spring but wither before the flower blooms in June. The white flowers form a spherical cluster about 1 to 2 inches wide on a single stem about 6 to 16 inches tall. Large stands of ramps can be seen in the Gravel Springs area. Rich in vitamins and minerals, the bulbs of ramps were traditionally eaten as a spring tonic. The tender young leaves can also be boiled and eaten. Those who have eaten ramps retain the pungent odor, and schools would occasionally have to close due to the overwhelming aroma in the classroom.

FLY POISON

Amianthium muscitoxicum
Bloom season: June–July
Bunchflower family (Melanthiaceae)
Height: 2–3′

In summer, Big Meadows is dotted with tall 2- to 3-foot-high spires of greenish-white flowers that wave their candlelike stems throughout the meadow. With long straplike leaves, fly poison is quite beautiful but deadly. The white flowers gradually turn greenish and then chartreuse-purple before they fade into dried brown spent torches. The plants often form large colonies throughout the park, especially in sandy or moist areas like Big Meadows. All parts of the plant contain toxic alkaloids. It was used by Native Americans to poison crows that attempted to damage their crops. The species name is from the Latin words *muscae,* for "flies," and *toxicum,* for "poison." Early settlers ground up the powdered root and mixed it with sugar water or molasses to kill flies in their homes.

PARTRIDGEBERRY

Mitchella repens
Bloom season: June–July
Madder family (Rubiaceae)
Height: 4–12″

Creeping along the ground, partridgeberry has rounded opposite leaves that are topped with 2 delightfully fuzzy white flowers that are joined at the base. One bright-red berry is produced from the 2 flowers and is one of the favorite foods of white-tailed deer and birds. Native American women would drink a tea made from the berries and leaves of the plant two to three weeks before childbirth to ease labor pains. The tea was also used medicinally for menstrual cramps, diarrhea, and urinary difficulties. Berries could be eaten as a snack or made into a jelly.

COW PARSNIP

Heracleum maximum

Bloom season: June–August

Carrot family (Apiaceae)

Height: 3–10′

The Hercules of the flower world, cow parsnip towers above all other flowers on sunny banks lining the Skyline Drive. The genus name, *Heracleum,* refers to the mythological hero. The tall, white, flat-topped flower heads resemble Queen Anne's lace blooms but often reach the size of dinner plates. The maplelike leaves can reach up to 2 feet across. The seeds were cooked into a soup and were also used to relieve gas. The young leaves and the peeled stems were cooked and eaten in spring. The mature hollow stem was chopped, dried, and used as a salt substitute when cooking foods.

INDIAN HEMP

Apocynum cannabinum
Bloom season: June–August
Dogbane family (Apocynaceae)
Height: 1–5′

These rangy plants with their small greenish-white flowers grow profusely in dense colonies in open meadows such as Naked Creek Overlook. Indian hemp was used for many medicinal purposes, including heart problems, but its most common use was as fiber. Harvested by Native Americans in fall, the stems were split open and the long fibrous threads peeled off. The women rolled the silky fibers on their laps, twisting them into string, which they often dyed various colors. Used as an all-purpose thread, cord, or twine, it was utilized to make strong ropes, bridles, fishing nets, and clothing. The thread was used to fashion warm blankets made of turkey feathers. After harvesting, the fields of Indian hemp were burned, resulting in taller, straighter stems the following year.

SPOTTED WINTERGREEN

Chimaphila maculata
Bloom season: June–August
Heath Family (Ericaceae)
Height: 4–10″

The white-striped evergreen leaves of spotted wintergreen are conspicuous year-round in dry woods in Shenandoah. The Greek name, *Chimaphila,* means "winter lover," as the dark green leaves and brown fruit capsule remain throughout the cold winter months. In summer the sweet-smelling waxy-looking white flowers nod from a spindly stem. Settlers to the area commonly called this plant rheumatism root, as they used it to treat rheumatism. Native Americans used it as a wash to treat cancer, ulcers, and ringworm.

MICHAUX'S CLIFF SAXIFRAGE

Hydatica petiolaris
Bloom season: June–August
Saxifrage family (Saxifragaceae)
Height: 4–15″

Even though saxifrage sounds like it should be equated with a musical instrument, the word actually means "stone breaker." The thin wispy stems of saxifrage are in no way strong enough to break rock, but because the plants grow on cliff faces and rock outcroppings, people thought they caused the cracks and crevices in the rocks where they bloom. Michaux's cliff saxifrage is found only in the Southern Appalachians. This saxifrage is named for André Michaux, a French botanist who explored much of the Appalachians in the late 1700s. Other common saxifrages in the park include lettuce saxifrage (*Micranthes micranthidifolia*) and early saxifrage (*M. virginiensis*).

INDIAN PIPE

Monotropa uniflora
Bloom season: June–September
Heath family (Ericaceae)
Height: 2–10″

Catching the eye of hikers through rich woods in the park, the waxy white flowers of Indian pipe rise mysteriously through the dank leaf litter. Although it resembles a mushroom in texture, Indian pipe is a true plant with a true flower, although it lacks the green pigment chlorophyll. The ghostlike flower hangs downward at first, but as the flower matures, it points its head upward and gradually turns black. A mycoparasite, the flower receives the nutrients it needs from fungi. Native Americans used the plant's juice as an eye drop. In September, colonists gathered the root and dried it to use as a treatment for nervous disorders.

YUCCA

Yucca filamentosa
Bloom season: June–September
Agave family (Agavaceae)
Height: 3–15'

The tall spikes of this yucca seem out of place in the park, as most yuccas are found in the deserts and grasslands of western North America. One species, *Yucca filamentosa,* or as it is commonly called, Adam's needle, is native to the East and Midwest. Other common names, including Spanish bayonet, Spanish dagger, Eve's thread, and soap root, all tend to describe the appearance or use of the plant. The large, nodding white flowers attract bees, moths, and hummingbirds. Native Americans peeled the leaves into long fibers and braided them into cords, baskets, and fishing nets. The roots were pounded, boiled, and used as washing soap. Look for this flower along Skyline Drive near the Old Rag Overlook.

BLACK COHOSH

Actaea racemosa
Bloom season: June–September
Buttercup family (Ranunculaceae)
Height: 3–8′

Summer motorists will notice tall white spikes of black cohosh along Skyline Drive. The blooms' rank odor attracts flies that pollinate the flower, but other insects avoid it, as the common name bugbane suggests. It is larval food for the Appalachian blue butterfly. Native Americans used the plant as an aid in childbirth and for female problems. Colonists used it to treat fevers, bronchitis, snakebite, and rheumatism. Also called black snakeroot, it was one of the many "snake oil" drugs sold as cure-alls by traveling salesmen. Today black cohosh is used as a dietary supplement for women. Current research suggests that it may be helpful for menopausal symptoms, but long-term safety data is not yet available.

TRAILING WHITE MONKSHOOD

Aconitum reclinatum
Bloom season: June–September
Buttercup family (Ranunculaceae)
Height: 2–8′

Trailing white monkshood is a rare plant found only in five eastern states. Listed as vulnerable or critically imperiled, it finds a refuge within the protected borders of Shenandoah National Park. Also known as trailing wolfsbane, members of the genus *Aconitum* have been of interest since ancient times because they contain toxins called alkaloids that can be deadly poisonous. These alkaloids were used medicinally in the United States until their use was discontinued in the early 1940s.

COMMON YARROW

Achillea millefolium
Bloom season: June–November
Aster family (Asteraceae)
Height: 1–3′

Known throughout the world, the unassuming white flat-topped heads of common yarrow are found garnishing the Skyline Drive and along trails throughout the park. Often confused with Queen Anne's lace, the feathery green fernlike leaves are useful in differentiating the two. The genus name, *Achillea*, honors Achilles, the Greek hero of the Trojan War, who carried leaves of yarrow into battle to heal his soldiers' arrow wounds. Civil War doctors also used the leaves to stop the bleeding of wounded soldiers, and pioneer homemakers kept the plant on hand to treat injuries. The leaves were chewed for toothaches and were used to treat hemorrhoids and dysentery.

AMERICAN GINSENG

Panax quinquefolius
Bloom season: July–August
Ginseng family (Araliaceae)
Height: 8–24″

Valued for centuries as a cure-all, ginseng played an important role in the lives of early settlers. Commonly called "sang," the plants were used for medicinal purposes, but in the Shenandoah area they were more often gathered as a much-needed cash crop. In the 1940s a pound of dried ginseng roots could be sold for about $8, which is the equivalent of about $120 today. The roots, which look like small, branched parsnips, resemble the shape of a human body, and it was believed that ginseng was good for all ailments; it was also used as an aphrodisiac. The genus name, *Panax,* honors the Greek goddess of cures, Panacea, who was one of the daughters of Asclepius, the Greek god of healing. This once-common plant is now listed as a threatened species in thirty-one states.

WINTERGREEN

Gaultheria procumbens
Bloom season: July–August
Heath family (Ericaceae)
Height: 2–6"

The thick oval leaves of this evergreen lie low against the forest floor throughout the park. Blooming in summer, the small white bell-shaped flowers hang beneath the leaves and are often overlooked. Sometimes described as "sealing-wax red," the dry berries that replace the flowers are often more noticeable, especially as they often last into the winter. Often called teaberry, the leaves were used to make a wintergreen-flavored tea. Early colonists used the tea medicinally to treat the aches of arthritis. Chipmunks and squirrels eat the berries in winter, and deer browse on the leaves.

DOWNY RATTLESNAKE PLANTAIN

Goodyera pubescens
Bloom season: July–August
Orchid family (Orchidaceae)
Height: 6–16″

This summer-blooming orchid has small white flowers that spiral up the flowering stalk. Though not a plantain at all, rattlesnake plantains get their name from their egg-shaped leaves, which are similar to the leaves of the common weed called plantain. The leaves are evergreen and heavily striped with whitish veins, forming a checkerboard pattern similar to snake skin. Its appearance is probably a cue to its use, as this plant was used for snakebites. If bitten, the victim would quickly locate rattlesnake plantain leaves; chew them, swallowing a bit of the juice; and then apply the chewed leaves to the bite. The plant was used by Native Americans and settlers for other medicinal treatments, including rheumatism, toothache, sore eyes, and scrofula, which was a common form of tuberculosis affecting the lymph nodes of the neck.

FRAGRANT BEDSTRAW

Galium triflorum

Bloom season: July–September

Madder family (Rubiaceae)

Height: 8–32"

The name bedstraw refers to the plant's historical use as stuffing for mattresses. It was also used to curdle milk to make cheese. Creeping on the ground or on other plants, the whorled leaves of fragrant bedstraw release a sweet odor like that of freshly mown hay. In the 1800s breast cancer was treated by drinking bedstraw juice and by applying the bruised leaves to the diseased area. Freckles could also be removed in this manner. Bedstraw was commonly used to make a tea and as a coffee substitute. In 1978 scientists discovered that the plant is toxic to the liver and kidneys, and today it is used only as an ingredient in mouse poison. Also found in the park, cleavers (*G. aparine*) is a related bedstraw a rough, prickled stem.

WHITE WOOD ASTER

Eurybia divaricata
Bloom season: July–October
Aster family (Asteraceae)
Height: 1–3′

The cluster of flat-topped white flowers of white wood aster seems to have a paucity of white ray flowers, which helps distinguish it from the more prolific flowers of similar species. The center flowers start out yellow then change to reddish purple as they age. This plant has undergone several name changes as botanists discovered through genetic research that many of the flowers that were originally placed in the *Aster* genus do not share common characteristics with true asters. The former Latin name for this plant was *Aster divaricatus,* but all new references place it in the genus *Eurybia,* along with similar plants, such as bigleaf aster (*E. macrophylla*) and low rough aster (*E. radula*). You'll find white wood aster in dry wooded areas of the park.

BONESET

Eupatorium perfoliatum
Bloom season: July–October
Aster family (Asteraceae)
Height: 2–5'

This plant is native to North America, and the first medicinal use of bonesets was for healing broken bones. This use was suggested by the plant's appearance because the opposite leaves join together around the stem. Having learned from Native Americans its medicinal use for fevers, early colonists gathered and dried the plant in the fall, hanging it in bundles for future use. Malaria was extremely common in the United States at the time. During the Civil War, malaria and other diseases killed more soldiers than did battle wounds. Not understanding that mosquitoes carried the disease, people blamed it on "swamp vapors." Peruvian bark, or quinine, was in short supply, so boneset, along with the bark of flowering dogwood, was made into a bitter tea to treat malaria victims.

HAIRY WHITE OLDFIELD ASTER

Symphyotrichum pilosum
Bloom season: August–October
Aster family (Asteraceae)
Height: 1–4′

Thriving from the valleys and hollows to the mountain meadows, hairy white oldfield aster brightens the Shenandoah landscape. Multitudes of white flowers decorate these robust plants with stems that spread like a flowing dress. Two types of flowers make up asters. The outer white daisy petal–like structures are called ray flowers. The inner yellow centers are the disk flowers. Like many asters, the disk flowers at the center of the flower's head open yellow then turns reddish after they are pollinated. The stems and leaves are extremely hairy, so much so that they have a frosty appearance, earning them another common name: frost aster.

YELLOW NODDING LADIES' TRESSES

Spiranthes ochroleuca
Bloom season: September–November
Orchid family (Orchidaceae)
Height: 6–12″

Often overlooked, the single stalks of ladies' tresses orchids feature spiraling tiny white flowers that seem to twinkle in the sunlight for those lucky enough to find them. Several species are found in Shenandoah, including southern slender ladies' tresses (*S. lacera*), nodding ladies' tresses (*S. cernua*), and yellow nodding ladies' tresses (*S. ochroleuca*). Yellow nodding ladies' tresses can be found blooming in Big Meadows from September to November.

Useful References

The following wildflower field guides offer further resources to deepen your knowledge and satisfy your curiosity about the wonderful world of wildflowers. The much anticipated *Flora of Virginia* is due to be published in 2012 and will cover all plants found in the state.

Clemants, S., and C. Gracie. *Wildflowers in the Field and Forest.* New York: Oxford University Press, 2006.

Digital Atlas of Virginia: www.biol.vt.edu/digital_atlas/.

Newcomb, L. *Newcomb's Wildflower Guide.* Boston: Little, Brown, and Company, 1977.

Peterson, R. T., and M. McKenny. *A Field Guide to Wildflowers Northeastern and North-central North America.* Boston: Houghton Mifflin Company, 1986.

Weakley, A. S. *Flora of the Southern and Mid-Atlantic States.* University of North Carolina at Chapel Hill: www.herbarium .unc.edu/flora.htm.

Butterfly milkweed brightens the summer in Big Meadows.

Glossary

Alkaloid: Bitter compounds produced by plants to discourage predators

Alternate leaves: Leaves growing singly on a stem without an opposite leaf

Anther: Tip of a flower's stamen that produces pollen grains

Basal: At the base

Bulb: Underground structure made up of layered, fleshy scales

Corm: Rounded, solid underground stem

Disk flower: Small tubular flowers at the center of a composite flower

Doctrine of Signatures: A 17th-century belief that plants display a sign that indicates its use medicinally

Endemic: Growing only in a specific region or habitat

Genus: Taxonomic rank below family and above species; always capitalized and italicized

Nectar: Sweet liquid produced by flowers to attract pollinators

Opposite leaves: Leaves growing in pairs along the stem

Ovary: Chamber at the bottom of the pistil where seeds develop

Perfoliate leaf: Leaf whose stem appears to pass through the leaf

Pistil: Female part of a flower that is made up of the stigma, style, and ovary

Pollen: Small powdery particles that contain the plant's male sex cells

Pollination: Transfer of pollen from an anther to a stigma

Ray flower: Petal-like flowers that surround a central group of disk flowers

Rhizome: Underground stem that grows horizontally and sends up shoots

Sepal: Leaf-like structures, usually green, found underneath the flower

Species: Taxonomic rank below genus; always italicized but never capitalized; also called "specific epithet"

Stamen: Male part of the flower composed of a filament, or stalk, and anther, the sac at the tip of the filament that produces pollen

Stigma: Sticky tip of the pistil that receives pollen

Style: Stalk-like part of the pistil that receives the pollen; connects the ovary and stigma

Toothed: Jagged or serrated edge

Whorled: Circle of three of more leaves encircling a stem

Winged: Thin, flattened expansion on the sides of a plant part

Index

About the Authors

As professional photographers, biologists, and authors, Ann and Rob Simpson are noted national park experts having spent years involved with research and interpretation in the national parks. They have written numerous books on national parks coast to coast that promote wise and proper use of natural habitats and environmental stewardship. As a former chief of interpretation and national park board member, Rob has a unique understanding of the inner workings of the national park system. In cooperation with American Park Network, they have led Canon "Photography in the Parks" workshops in major national parks including Grand Canyon, Yellowstone, Yosemite, and Great Smokies.

Ann and Rob are both award-winning biology professors at Lord Fairfax Community College in Middletown, Virginia. With a background in science education, Ann heads the science department and as part of the college's nature photography curriculum, the Simpson's regularly lead international photo tours to parks and natural history destinations around the world.

Long known for their stunning images of the natural world, their work has been widely published in magazines such as *National Geographic, Time Magazine, National Wildlife,* and *Ranger Rick* as well as many calendars, postcards, and books. You can see their work at Simpson's Nature Photography at www .agpix.com/snphotos.